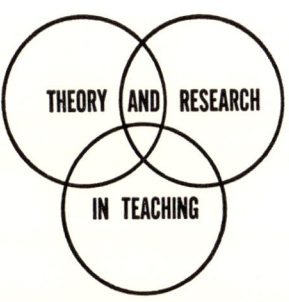

Teachers College, Columbia University
Arno A. Bellack, editor

Recent years have witnessed a resurgence of interest on the part of educational researchers in the teaching process. Volumes in the *Theory and Research in Teaching* series report significant studies of instructional procedures in a variety of educational settings, at various organizational levels in the schools, and in many of the subjects included in the curriculum. These studies present fresh perspectives on teaching both to educational researchers and to practitioners in the schools.

# The Teacher Moves

## AN ANALYSIS OF NON-VERBAL ACTIVITY

---

**Barbara M. Grant**
**Dorothy Grant Hennings**

**Teachers College Press**
Teachers College, Columbia University
New York, New York

Copyright © 1971 by Teachers College, Columbia University
Library of Congress Catalog Card Number: 71-148592

Manufactured in the United States of America

to our mother and father, with love

# Foreword

As a result of the burgeoning interest during recent years in the study of classroom teaching, we are beginning to accumulate a substantial body of information about life in classrooms. To date, research on teaching has focused primarily on verbal communication between teachers and students; little attention has been given to the non-verbal actions of classroom participants. Yet anyone who has been in classrooms either as observer or participant knows full well that communication between teachers and students takes place through non-verbal means (gestures, facial expressions, body motions, and the like) as well as through verbal means. The study by Barbara Grant and Dorothy Hennings reported in this volume is significant because it is one of the first investigations to shed light on some of the non-verbal dimensions of classroom interaction. Through studying teaching behavior recorded on video tapes, the authors provide a description of what they refer to as "teacher motions." A distinctive feature of their study is the development of a framework for analysis that enables them to relate in pedagogically meaningful ways non-verbal and verbal components of classroom discourse.

The authors' exploration of non-verbal aspects of communication in elementary school classrooms enlarges our understanding of the teaching process by providing us with a description of features of that process that have thus far been largely neglected by researchers.

Arno A. Bellack

# Acknowledgments

We acknowledge with sincere thanks the cooperation given by the many teachers and student teachers whose classroom behavior we have observed and used as a source of ideas. We particularly acknowledge the contribution made by the five teachers whose behavior we studied in detail. Without the first-hand data obtained from these sources, this book would not have been possible.

Our appreciation is extended to Professor Arno Bellack of Teachers College, Columbia University, who read and commented on the manuscript, and to Professor Rosedith Sitgreaves, also of Teachers College, Columbia University, who gave statistical advice. We also acknowledge Professor George Hennings of Newark State College, who helpfully criticized the original draft of this book; Mr. William Grant, who assisted with statistical calculations; and Mr. Stanley Wollock, who designed the cover for *The Teacher Moves*.

B. M. G.
D. G. H.

# Contents

Foreword by *Arno A. Bellack*     vii

Acknowledgments     ix

*Part I*
*Describing the Way the Teacher Moves*

CHAPTER 1
A Description Based on Research     3

CHAPTER 2
Motions and the Teacher     8

CHAPTER 3
Teacher Motions and the Instructional Process     25

CHAPTER 4
Teacher Motions and Teaching Style     42

*Part II*
*Improving the Way Teachers Move*

CHAPTER 5
Experimenting with Non-verbal Strategies     63

CHAPTER 6
Generating Non-verbal Clues     73

CHAPTER 7
Factors Related to the Production of Non-verbal Clues     81

CHAPTER 8
Selecting from Among Non-verbal Options     90

CHAPTER 9
Improving Teaching Via Descriptive Research:
A Point of View     107

Bibliography     109

APPENDIX A
> Statistical Tables 115

APPENDIX B
> An Inventory for Analyzing Non-verbal Teacher Activity 125

# The Teacher Moves

## PART I

*Describing the Way
the Teacher Moves*

Chapter 1

# A Description Based on Research

A girl lowers her head. A mother pats her baby's leg. A workman wipes the sweat from his brow. A young man slips his arm around his girl. A demonstrator rapidly waves a sign. How are all these situations interrelated? In the context of the particular situations in which these people are interacting, they are communicating meaning through their physical acts. The girl may be communicating embarrassment; the mother and the young man may be saying, "I care." The demonstrator may be communicating belief in a cause, whereas the workman may be saying non-verbally, "I am hot."

In everyday encounters between persons non-verbal activity does communicate meanings. Often what is done in face-to-face interaction has greater meaning than what is said verbally; a small motion of the hand, a stretching of the torso, a jerking of the foot, a shrug of the shoulders tell the listener as much as or more than the accompanying words.

To communicate a specific nuance, the speaker intentionally uses a gesture of the hand or a motion of the head; this gesture or motion may reinforce what the speaker is saying or may give added meaning to the words. Sometimes the speaker communicates solely at the non-verbal level; wordlessly—with a look or with an almost imperceptible movement of the body—a message is sent.

## MOTION IN TEACHING

Because the teacher is vitally concerned with the communication of meanings, in the encounter between teacher and student physical motions are even more significant than in the non-structured encounter between persons. Although the teacher communicates at the verbal level by answering student questions, by projecting questions, and by reacting with a positive "Yes" or a negative "No," he communicates non-verbally by pointing, by nodding his head, by holding up his hands, by walking toward a student.

The importance of non-verbal motion in teaching shows up in even brief samples of teaching. For example, in a very short time sequence, one teacher:

> walked away from the board and toward the children,
> opened a book,
> looked down at a question in the planbook,
> placed his left hand on the open book,
> looked up at the children in the class,
> looked down at the book to check the question,
> walked back to board,
> looked up at children,
> closed book on finger,
> brought up hand to write on board,
> wrote "you" on board,
> underlined the word, and
> turned toward the class.

During this sequence of actions, the teacher made only two remarks: "Now let's take this one," and "What verb is always used with 'you'— always used with 'you' in the present tense?" Most of his activity was non-verbal.

During a comparable sequence a second teacher made only one remark: "Can anyone think of another word that rhymes with 'hill'?" Non-verbally he (1) looked at the class group, (2) moved his head to survey the group, (3) pointed to a particular child, and (4) wrote the word on the easel. A major aspect of this teacher's performance was similarly non-verbal.

Yet when we look at descriptions of teaching, we find little that indicates the role played by non-verbal teacher activity. Many questions remain unanswered. What kinds of non-verbal motions do teachers use? What do teachers' motions mean in terms of pedagogical functioning? How does non-verbal teacher activity relate to verbal activity? What do the non-verbal motions of a teacher tell us about the unique style of that teacher?

## GATHERING DATA ON MOTION IN TEACHING [1]

It was to answer these and related questions that we developed a category system to describe teacher motion reliably and went into the classroom both with observers in an informal approach and with videotaping cameras in a more systematic, statistical approach. We applied this two-track technique (1) to see if the category system we had designed could produce statistically reliable information about ways teachers move and (2) to see if teachers-in-training could apply this system in informal classroom observations.

The informal approach relied on undergraduate education students, who observed as part of a junior sequence of professional courses. These students went into classrooms and first recorded in anecdotal fashion teachers' physical motions. Since more than one observer went into each class session, it was possible to cross-check actions. The students were then introduced to a concept of instructional and personal motions and to different kinds of instructional motions—conducting, acting, and wielding. Next they looked at the motions they had observed in terms of these categories. The students worked in a similar fashion with categories related to moves and move patterns. From their observations, some general ideas emerged about the way teachers use motion in their classrooms.

The systematic, more formal approach relied on video-tape recordings of lessons. Two portable cameras were employed, one in the front and one in the back of a classroom. The cameras were placed on pedestals located approximately seven feet above the floor and were equipped with microphones and zoom lenses. Each of the cameras was connected to a console in a recording studio, from which the technician could focus the cameras and film by remote control. With this equipment, a technician had no difficulty filming teachers or picking up their voices; he was able to zoom in on a teacher recording finer body motions and to pan the classroom keeping up with grosser motions. Because the equipment had been functioning for a period of one year prior to filming and because the teachers' motions had been followed with remote-controlled cameras on many previous occasions, their performances were probably little affected by the video taping.

[1] Barbara M. Grant, "A Method for Analyzing the Non-verbal Behavior (Physical Motions) of Teachers of Elementary School Language Arts" (unpublished doctoral dissertation, Teachers College, Columbia University, 1969). The development of the category system, the filming of the lessons for analysis, and the statistical analysis of the data occurred as a part of this study.

The use of video-tape recordings as a basis for studying non-verbal teaching has certain advantages over techniques involving lower levels of technology. First, video-taping cameras pick up both sound and physical motion. This makes possible the study of interrelationships between verbal and non-verbal teaching behavior. Second, the number of non-verbal motions a teacher makes in even a small unit of time can be rather high. To record these motions accurately in a written log made on the spot lowers the reliability of descriptions about non-verbal teaching. With video tape we can view and review classroom episodes. Third, as several observers view a video tape, they can discuss how a particular motion is being used in a classroom while actually looking at that motion. On the other hand, if these researchers are sitting in a classroom observing the way the teacher moves, resolution of conflicting notions cannot occur. The teacher himself can also see the final tapes and indicate why he was making certain motions.

## A CASE STUDY APPROACH

Applying these techniques, we focused our lenses on the classroom performance of five experienced and well-prepared teachers in a case study approach. These teachers—all in their late twenties—can be considered experienced; each had been in the classroom a minimum of three years at the time his behavior was observed. The men and women teachers represented grades one through five.

Although the school in which these teachers taught was a demonstration school associated with a state college, the classes were not atypical. There were approximately thirty pupils in each class. The students came from various backgrounds: urban, suburban, and semi-rural; upper socio-economic, middle, and lower. Likewise, the ability range was rather broad, and differences in interests and values existed among the students.

For each teacher five twenty-minute lessons were recorded. From each lesson, a two-minute episode or segment was randomly selected for detailed consideration. In addition, two two-minute segments were selected from one lesson of each teacher. These data were then translated into written typescripts in which (1) all teacher verbal activity was recorded and (2) all physical motions were described.

Working from these scripts, four coders analyzed the motions the teachers had employed. The coders were primarily undergraduate students trained in the use of the category system; they had previously studied data utilizing other systems of analysis and they had spent considerable time identifying motions on video-tape recordings. It was these data, amassed by the coders, that were studied statistically and that were utilized as a research base for descriptions of how teachers move.

Chapter 2

# *Motions and the Teacher*

Turn off the audio in a classroom, and observe a teacher in action. The teacher pulls down a map . . . points to a location on the map . . . adjusts his glasses . . . points to a child to respond . . . shakes his head . . . scratches his chin in a way typically his own . . . moves to the chalkboard . . . picks up a piece of chalk . . . again scratches his chin in that typical way . . . points with the chalk to a second child . . . nods . . . writes the word "China" on the board . . . moves away from the board . . . turns back to the board to dot the "i" . . . drops the chalk . . . slips his hand into his pocket . . . takes his hand out of his pocket to straighten his jacket . . . puts his hand back into his pocket . . . walks toward a child in the front row . . . picks up the child's paper . . . adjusts his own glasses . . . looks at the paper . . . holds the paper so that the child can see it . . . points to a word on the paper . . . shakes his head . . . .

Turn down the volume in a second classroom. There a teacher perches in a relaxed way on the edge of a desk. He looks down at a book in his hand . . . looks up . . . nods to a student . . . then nods to a second student . . . moves his right hand from a position on his hip to the corner of the book . . . turns the page . . . scratches his ear . . . puts his hand back on his hip . . . nods to a third child . . . .

Even the most casual, untrained observer can note differences in the kinds of motions these teachers employ, in the purposes for which they use physical motion, and in the meanings they are trying to communicate non-verbally. The trained researcher, using a classification system, is at the opposite end of a continuum; he can analyze such differences with a high degree of reliability. The classroom teacher who has understanding of how motions can be used in the classroom can go beyond even the trained observer; he can learn to produce sequences of motions that add to rather than detract from his verbal teaching.

## INSTRUCTIONAL AND PERSONAL MOTIONS

What are the kinds of motions a teacher uses? Research evidence indicates that teacher motion can be reliably classed as instructional or personal. When categorizing was done by student teachers trained in the use of the two categories, reliability coefficients of .94 to .99 were obtained. These high coefficients seem to suggest that use of the two categories—instructional and personal—is one positive way to look at non-verbal teaching.

### *Instructional Motions*

What is an instructional motion? When the teacher in the example above pulls down the map, picks up the chalk to write on the board, or turns the page of a book, he is readying his materials for teaching. When he points to the map or writes the word "China" on the board, he is focusing the attention of his students. When he points or nods to a child, he may be asking, "Jack, what is the answer?" Each of these motions is instructional because it facilitates teaching. Each is part of a sequence through which the teacher is guiding students in their learning.

Instructional motions are as integral a part of the teaching act as are verbal components. They communicate meanings that are essential in teaching. Motions may "say": "Look here!" "Very good, Susan." "*This* is the important part." "Be quiet!" "Let's get ready." "Let's hurry." "You're next." "*This* is what I mean." "This is what it looks like."

Although instructional motions are integral parts of teaching sequences, these motions are not necessarily performed consciously by the teacher. The teacher may have learned "pointing" to such an extent that this motion has become a natural component of his repertoire of motions; he uses his body without being totally aware of what he is doing.

Of course, many instructional motions are performed consciously by the teacher. The teacher who walks over to the light switch and flicks the lights to get attention is using a device that is part of the stock-in-trade of a teacher. Likewise, the primary school teacher, who reaches for a piece of chalk and breaks it in two before writing, is acting on a principle; she does not want the chalk to squeak.

### Personal Motions

How do these motions differ from those that can be called personal? The teacher scratches his ear, puts his hand into his pocket and then takes it out, tugs on his newly sprouting goatee, straightens his jacket, adjusts his glasses. His female equivalent, meanwhile, is playing with her pendant necklace, twisting her engagement ring, adjusting her skirt as she sits down on a low chair, tucking her hair back behind her ear. All of these motions are personal or self-adjusting because they are aspects of the teacher's humanness; they are not employed directly to aid in the learning process.

At times, the teacher uses personal, self-adjusting motions to achieve a more balanced state; he uses them to release tension and to achieve a more relaxed or comfortable bodily position. For instance, he may cross his legs, uncross his legs, lean back in his chair, straighten his body, drop his hand down to his side, clasp his hands, place his elbow on the desk, prop himself against the desk, sit down on a chair. He may put his hands into his pockets, rest his face on his hand, tap his finger on the desk, fan himself with a piece of paper.

Similarly, the teacher may use personal motions in adjusting articles on his body for social or practical purposes. The female teacher who adjusts her short skirt is employing bodily motion for this purpose as is the teacher who adjusts his glasses before looking at a student's paper. Teachers have been recorded on video-tape in the process of adjusting an earring that has fallen off and a slip strap that has fallen down; they have been recorded pulling down a sweater that has ridden up and placing a bobby pin back in the hair.

To some extent, motions may also be symptoms of inner conditions—a cold, a headache, a preoccupation with something else, a momentary itch; to some extent they may be indicative of a transition or change in mood. The teacher rubs the back of his neck, scratches his cheek, takes out a handkerchief, blows his nose, rubs his eye.

Bodily actions known as mannerisms fall into the personal category. We can all remember a teacher who showed marked or excessive adherence to a particular way of using his body—the one who was always twisting his arm behind his neck to scratch, the one who continually was winding his watch, the one who seemed never to stop pacing back and forth, the one who repeatedly pushed back her bangs.

The percentage of personal motions used in a classroom is amazingly high when one considers that such bodily action does not necessarily contribute positively to the instructional process. Of all the motions used by our case study teachers, 22.1 per cent were personal, and 77.9

per cent were instructional. The verbal equivalents of such personal motions are not that frequent. Teachers do remark: "I am tired." "Opps, I'm going to sneeze." "Excuse me." "Oh dear, I dropped my earring." Yet classroom observation of teachers uncovered only several instances of such verbal, personal actions.

## LOOKING AT INSTRUCTIONAL MOTIONS

Through studying teacher behavior recorded on video tape, we have identified three categories of instructional motions—conducting, acting, and wielding. Student teachers using these categories have been able to analyze teacher motions with a high degree of reliability; reliability coefficients ranged from .97 to .94. (See Appendix, Table A-1.) This section describes each of the categories.

### *1.0 Conducting*

A teacher physically conducts a class by involving one, some, or all of his students in the lesson. In conducting he uses motions that enable him to control student participation and obtain attending behavior.

***1.1 Controlling Participation.*** Physical motions *control participation* by focusing attention on materials, objects, persons, or even symbolic representations. These motions also indicate who the participants should be, when they should participate, and for how long; in a sense they halt or exclude interaction, elicit a physical response, rate a response, or answer the verbal or non-verbal inquiries of students. In addition, the motions regulate the flow, speed, and intensity of the verbal interaction. Examples, taken from actual classroom performances, are:

> moving the head to survey the group
> pointing to a child to begin
> turning to focus on a child
> pointing the microphone from a tape recorder at a child to indicate begin
> using index finger to connect one child's remarks to another child's
> leaning forward toward a child
> cocking head in a questioning way
> cupping hand behind ear
> shrugging shoulders
> raising hand to communicate "Would you raise your hand when you want to speak?"

***1.2 Obtaining Attending Behavior.*** *Obtaining attending behavior* is another aspect of the conducting act. Motions that obtain attending behavior usually occur prior to the launching of a lesson or during a transitional period within the lesson. They tend to vary from teacher to teacher; but in essence, they are all used for the same purpose—to acquire a spreading stillness or period of tranquility when every eye is focused on the teacher. Such motions are also used to gain the attention of a child who is misbehaving or a group of children who are not conforming to the established behavior pattern. Some examples are:

> clapping hands to gain the attention of the group
> tapping bell
> playing a note on the piano
> placing finger to lips
> holding up hand toward child to indicate: stop misbehaving
> clicking the light switch
> touching child on shoulder
> walking toward front of the room and standing still
> holding up hand to class group: quiet down
> pushing down start button for recording purposes: please be quiet because we are recording

That conducting motions can occur in repetitive patterns is evident. A cycle may get under way with the tapping of a bell to obtain attending behavior. The tap may be followed by surveying, pointing, nodding motions. Such a sequence can be repeated over and over again during a lesson.

### 2.0 Acting

A teacher uses bodily motion to amplify and clarify meanings he is trying to communicate. These motions emphasize or illustrate; in combination they also enable a teacher to make meanings more clear by the complete acting out of words, concepts, or objects, as in role playing and pantomime.

***2.1 Emphasizing.*** To *emphasize* a word or group of words a teacher may move his hand as he says the important words. He may swing his head to give emphasis to a word as when he says "No!" to a child. Sometimes he may move his entire torso, as when he moves his body to emphasize the rhythmic flow of language. And sometimes he may gesture with a microphone, chalk, or pointer to emphasize one aspect of the lesson. Some examples are:

> moving finger up and down as he speaks

giving head a sharp jerk
moving hand as he says word

**2.2 Illustrating.** To *illustrate* a teacher may use his hands to describe non-verbally some word, concept, or object under consideration. For instance, a teacher may move his hand in a circular pattern to describe what is meant by a spiral; he may point to indicate a direction in which the class should walk. Examples of illustrating are:

showing the movement of the wind
showing the size or shape of an object
indicating what time it is
counting the numbers on his fingers
illustrating concepts such as "to go away from" and "to go up"
referring to someone who has previously spoken

**2.3 Role Playing or Pantomiming.** In a third type of acting, *role playing or pantomiming*, the teacher actually pretends to be an object, an animal, or a character. In this respect his entire body gets into the act. Examples of possible role playing motions are:

taking on the role of an announcer
imitating a tiger
pretending to be a wilting daisy or a flat tire
hopping like the bunny in the story
playing dead

Although acting motions aid in the communication of meanings in the classroom, they also serve as interest-provoking devices; and because they do engender interest, they may enable a teacher to maintain student attention after attention has been gained through conducting motions. As a result of this dual function, acting motions serve a valuable purpose in the classroom.

### 3.0 Wielding

The teacher interacts with objects, materials, or parts of the room by using wielding motions.

**3.1 Direct Wielding.** A teacher may wield directly by touching, handling, or maneuvering "things" in the class. He *wields directly* when he is:

picking up book, pen, pencil, pointer, etc.
flipping pages in book

placing cover on the back of felt pen
adjusting shades in the classroom
placing globe on floor
holding down rewind button on tape recorder
placing book in lap
using eraser to erase board
writing words for his own use on paper while sitting at desk
writing sentences on board to be used later in the lesson as an exercise or assignment

**3.2 Indirect Wielding.** A teacher may *wield indirectly* by surveying, scanning, looking at, or reading things in the classroom environment; in this instance, the teacher does not come into direct bodily contact with the materials, but rather makes motions as he brings his eyes to a point where they can focus on some written or concrete material. A teacher wields indirectly when he is:

surveying or scanning books on shelf
standing in front of bookshelf looking for a particular book
looking down at book to read sentence
dropping head toward book to check answer
leaning over books on shelf to select book
glancing at clock to check time
looking down at watch to check time

**3.3 Instrumental Wielding.** The teacher also wields when he makes motions that enable him to interact with the physical environment of the classroom. These motions involve movement toward objects, materials, or part of the room. Because these motions are instrumental to the actual maneuvering of objects or materials, they can be called *instrumental wieldings;* a teacher wields instrumentally when he is:

walking back to desk
walking over to bookshelf
turning to write an assignment on easel or board for use later on in the lesson
walking over to tape recorder to turn off the machine

All wielding motions are not necessarily carried through to a logical, intended end. For instance, a teacher may begin to walk toward the tape recorder in a motion that would be classified as "instrumental to wielding" but never get to complete the action and turn on the recorder. Some other classroom event or a simple change of mind may interfere with the completion of the task. All wieldings, therefore, are not productive in terms of carrying the teaching step by step to an end point; some wieldings might even be considered abortive.

Just because a teacher's body comes into contact with an object does not mean that his motion involves a wielding act. A teacher often comes into physical contact with objects in the environment when he is conducting, especially when he is controlling participation. When he touches the chalkboard just beneath a word written there, he may be focusing attention on that particular word; and thus it is a conducting act he is performing rather than a wielding act.

### The Meaning of Motions

Throughout this discussion, it probably has become obvious to the reader that the motions of a teacher take on meaning only within the context in which they occur. For instance, a pointing of the finger does not always mean the same thing. Depending on the context, a pointing motion may mean:

> Let's go this way.
> Be quiet, Tracey.
> You recite, Wendy.
> This is the item we will take next.
> Look here.

Likewise, with a nod. A nod may mean:

> Good response.
> This is the end of the lesson.
> Interesting!
> What is the answer, Frank?
> Yes, you may leave the room.

What in one instance may be a motion used to control participation in another case may be a motion that obtains attending behavior, in another a motion that emphasizes, and in still another a motion that wields. One must look at the actual instructional setting to determine the meaning communicated.

## FACIAL EXPRESSIONS

So far little has been said about the teacher's facial expressions, and yet the facial muscles of most teachers are in a continual state of motion. Teachers smile, frown, grimace, wrinkle their foreheads, pull up their noses, squint, bite their tongues, make a "long face," grin, smirk, beam, and even wiggle their ears.

### Instructional Motions

Classroom observations of teaching behavior as well as study of video tapes of classroom action indicate that teachers use movement of facial muscles in much the same way as they use other bodily motions. Many of a teacher's facial expressions are related to the instructional process and can be categorized as conductings, actings, and wieldings.

In using facial conductings to control participation, the teacher:

> smiles at a child, meaning "You answer."
> grins at a child, meaning "We're on the right track."
> smiles at the entire class, meaning "Let's begin."
> beams from ear to ear, meaning "Excellent."
> wrinkles his forehead, meaning "Let's think about that again."

In using facial conductings to obtain attending behavior, the teacher:

> frowns at a child, meaning "Stop fooling around."
> raises his eyebrows, meaning "Pay attention."
> squints at a child, meaning "What are you up to back there?"

In using facial actings to emphasize, the teacher:

> opens his eyes wide on an important statement, indicating "This is significant."
> opens his mouth wider as he says an important word.

In using facial actings to illustrate, the teacher:

> puts on a downcast expression while reading a story to show "This is how the child felt."
> puffs up mouth and blows out to illustrate "This is the wind."

In using facial actings to pantomime or role play, the teacher:

> puckers up his mouth and "pulls down" his eyes to show "This is what the evil troll looked like."
> puffs out his cheek to make himself look like a chipmunk.

In using facial expressions to wield, the teacher:

> squints to read a title on the shelf.
> twitches his eye as he reads.

### Personal Motions

Facial motions not only are instructionally oriented but also are personal, self-adjusting. The most significant of these motions are those that fall into the category of mannerisms—motions that are repeated incessantly and often are distracting to a listener: the licking or biting of the lips, the clenching of the teeth accompanied by a tightening of cheek muscles.

Not all self-adjusting motions of the face are mannerisms. Just as in the case of other motions, facial expressions can be a reaction to inner conditions or means of adjusting articles on one's body. The teacher who sniffs his nose may be suffering from a cold; the one who wiggles his nose may have a passing itch. Then again that wiggle of the nose may be a way of pushing up one's eye glasses, which have slipped down.

### Analyzing Facial Expressions

To study facial expressions even with video-taping procedures is an almost impossible task. First, it is often difficult at a distance to determine whether a teacher's expression is a grimace or a frown, a smile or a beam. Then too facial expressions are more a continual state of being—happy, sad, in-between, or even a mask of inner feeling. For these reasons, we have not analyzed facial expressions using statistical techniques and we did not include them in any mathematical interpretation of teaching. Rather we looked at these motions separately in a rather subjective way.

This is not to suggest that facial expressions are an insignificant part of teaching. Just the opposite is true. The expression on a teacher's face may reassure a child, set the climate for the day, or even irritate another child. A child can "read" a teacher's expression, "Miss Jackson is in a bad mood today" and translate that into his own behavior, "I'd better watch out." Or conversely, "Miss Jackson is in a good mood—she won't send me to the office today!"

## MOTION IN THE CLASSROOM

What is the teacher doing when he teaches? At the physical level, he is performing as a conductor, using gestures and motions that often bear a striking resemblance to the gestures and motions of a musical conductor. The teacher is also performing as an actor, building interest and clarifying meanings with his body. In addition, he is performing as a technician, wielding aspects of the environment. Finally, the teacher is performing as a human being, bringing with him into the classroom personal motions that do not have an instructional purpose. Each of the categories of physical motion is, thus, based on a nonverbal teaching role.

Although the teacher performs non-verbally as conductor, actor, technician, and person, he does not play each role in equal proportions. It has already been noted that of all the motions used by a sample of teachers, 77.9 per cent were instructional, 22.1 per cent were personal. In the same pilot study on which this book is based, it was also discovered that in the sample group of case study teachers certain instructional motions tend to predominate. The relative proportion of motion types is shown below in Table 1.

Analysis of these data reveals that this restricted population of case study teachers used more "conducting" motions than "acting" or "wielding" motions. These teachers as a group used very few "acting" motions. Within the conducting category the teachers primarily employed motions that controlled student participation in the learning situation; relatively few motions (less than six per cent) were used to obtain attending behavior. Of course, the teachers in this population were highly experienced. The new teacher might find himself using a greater number of such motions.

## A SIMPLE DESIGN FOR LOOKING AT TEACHER ACTIVITY

Let us now look at a typical classroom episode and analyze the kinds of motions the teacher is using. In so doing we shall consider each of the physical motions in terms of the categories already developed.

TABLE 1. How the Teacher Moves

| | | |
|---|---|---|
| 1.0 Conducting | | 62.5% |
| 1.1 Controlling Participation | 57.04% | |
| 1.2 Obtaining Attending Behavior | 5.47% | |
| 2.0 Acting | | 8.8% |
| 2.1 Emphasizing | 4.25% | |
| 2.2 Illustrating | 4.45% | |
| 2.3 Role Playing or Pantomiming | .05% | |
| 3.0 Wielding | | 28.7% |
| 3.1 Direct Wielding | 11.63% | |
| 3.2 Indirect Wielding | 7.87% | |
| 3.3 Instrumental Wielding | 9.24% | |

## The Framework

***Instructional Motions.*** This category comprises motions that deal with teaching purposes and processes.
    1.0 Conducting: Motions that enable the teacher to control the participation and obtain attending behavior of students. These motions serve to involve the students either verbally or non-verbally.
        1.1 Controlling participation
        1.2 Obtaining attending behavior
    2.0 Acting: Motions that enable the teacher to clarify and amplify meanings by holding the attention of students.
        2.1 Emphasizing (word or group of words)
        2.2 Illustrating (words or concepts)
        2.3 Role playing or pantomiming (objects, animals, characters)
    3.0 Wielding: Motions through which the teacher interacts with aspects of the physical environment—objects, materials, or parts of the room.
        3.1 Direct wielding (touching, handling, maneuvering)
        3.2 Indirect wielding (scanning, looking at, reading: motions made in)
        3.3 Instrumental Wielding (movement toward)

***Personal Motions.*** This category comprises motions that deal with human purposes and processes.

## The Episode

Here is a fifth grade lesson in which the teacher is developing the concept of what a noun is. His physical motions are indicated on the right. His verbal motions are given at the left. The children's comments are noted in the center column to make the meanings of the action clearer to the reader.

During this episode the teacher makes more than forty physical motions. Yet, it is obvious to anyone who has concentrated on study of teacher motions that the number of physical motions is not abnormally high. Teachers in practice tend to be active—perhaps because teaching involves the use of audio-visual, concrete materials: chalkboards, projectors, pens, pencils, paper, books, etc.; perhaps because teaching involves keeping students' attention focused on the subject; perhaps because teaching involves housekeeping tasks: answering telephones, arranging window blinds, opening and closing windows.

| The teacher says | The children say | The teacher moves |
| --- | --- | --- |
| | | Walks to the board |
| | | Picks up the chalk |
| | | Tries to write with the chalk but finds it doesn't work |
| | | Looks down at it |
| | | Tries to write with the chalk |
| | | Drops it into the tray |
| | | Picks up another |
| | | Writes on board "The *quaq* is a *floop*." |
| Can someone give me real words to put in this sentence? Leslie? | | Turns to the class |
| | | Brushes hand against nose |
| | | Pushes up glasses |
| | | Surveys class |
| | | Points to child |
| | Leslie says: "The dog is a collie." | |
| Yes. | | Nods |
| | | Turns to the board |
| | | Writes dog under *quaq* |
| | | Writes collie under *floop* |
| | | Turns back to the class |
| Another? | | Walks toward Fred, who is not paying attention |
| | | Waves hand at him |
| | | Surveys class |
| | | Points to another child whose hand is raised |
| | Jack says: "The car is a Ford." | |
| That's right Jack, "The car is a Ford." | | Uses hand as he talks to stress car and Ford |
| | | Walks back to the board |
| | | Writes car under dog |
| | | Writes Ford under collie |
| | | Walks to desk |
| | | Picks up open book |
| | | Scans the page to find another sentence |
| Let's look at this sentence next. | | Returns to the board |
| | | Writes on the board: "The *drikle* gave us some *lacks*." |
| Read this sentence and substitute real words for *drikle* and *lacks*. | | Turns to the class |
| | | Pumps hand on *drikle* and *lacks* |
| | | Surveys group |
| | | Nods at Tracey |
| | "The butcher gave us some meat." | |
| | | Turns to the board |
| | | Writes "butcher" under "drikle" |

## Motions and the Teacher    21

| The teacher says | The children say | The teacher moves |
|---|---|---|
| | | Writes "meat" under "lacks" |
| | | Surveys class |
| Frank? | "The cow gave us some milk." | |
| | | Writes "cow" under "butcher" |
| | | Writes "milk" under "meat" |
| | | Drops the chalk |
| | | Turns to the class |
| | | Pulls down his sweater |
| Let's look at all the words which you have given me: dog, collie, car, Ford, butcher, meat, cow, milk | | Folds arms |
| | | Unfolds arms |
| | | Moves finger up and down as he says each word in the sequence |
| | | Moves finger against nose |
| What are all these words? | | Points toward Alex |
| | | Walks toward Fred |
| | | Shakes head at Fred |

    What kinds of motions does this teacher make? First, the teacher makes a number of motions that are clearly personal, self-adjusting acts. When the teacher brushes his hand against his nose, he is reacting to some internal bodily condition. When he pushes up his glasses and pulls down his sweater, he is simply adjusting a part of his clothing for practical reasons. When he folds and unfolds his arms, he is taking on a new bodily stance as a means of relaxing.

    The other motions he makes are related to the instructional process. As the teacher walks to the board at the beginning of the sequence, the children are expected to follow along with his motions; the motions focus the children's attention. These motions are part of the conducting act, specifically controlling participation. The same can be said of most of the initial motions, other than the interaction with the chalk:

    walks to the board
    tries to write
    tries to write again
    writes on the board "The *quaq* is a *floop*."

The following motions can also be considered in that category:

    points to Leslie
    nods
    turns to board
    writes

turns back to class
points to another child.

In the next sequence within the episode the teacher uses conducting motions to obtain attending behavior:

walks toward Fred, who is not paying attention
waves hand at him.

These motions communicate to Fred: "I know that you are not paying attention. Stop that!"

On several occasions the teacher uses hand motions that can be considered acting–emphasizing:

uses hand as he talks to stress car and Ford
pumps hand on "drikle" and "lack"
moves finger up and down as he says each word.

These motions add meaning to the utterances they accompany; they clarify what is being said.

The next sequence of motions is again an attempt to control participation by conducting:

walks back to the board
writes car under dog, Ford under collie.

These are conducting motions that focus attention because students are supposed to follow these motions.

On the other hand, when the teacher walks to the desk to check the book to determine what the next example will be, the students are not expected to follow his motions. The motions, therefore, are not conducting activities. Rather he is wielding:

walks to desk (instrumental wielding)
picks up book (direct wielding)
scans the page for another word (indirect wielding).

The motion of walking to the desk is instrumental to wielding, for it gets the teacher in a position to wield. The picking up of the book is a direct wielding, for it involves the actual maneuvering of an object. The scanning of the page is an indirect wielding; it involves motions made as the eyes are used to read.

If we return to the introductory sequence of motions, we note some additional "direct wieldings":

picks up chalk
drops chalk
picks up another piece of chalk.

There is also an indirect wielding:

> looks at chalk.

These again are wieldings, for the students are not expected to focus on the chalk. When he tries to use the chalk to write, however, that is a different situation; he expects the students to focus on his activity and, therefore, is controlling participation.

Most of the remaining motions are conductings to control participation:

> returns to board
> writes on board "The drikle gave us some lacks."
> turns to class
> nods at Tracey
> turns to board
> writes "butcher"
> writes "cow"
> turns to class
> points to Alex.

Each of these motions focuses attention on the subject of the lesson or identifies participants.

The final motions involving Fred are disciplinary and are to obtain attending behavior:

> walks toward Fred
> shakes head at Fred.

### Analysis of Episode

Within this episode the use of the body in the instructional process is rather typical of teacher performance in a discussion situation. The teacher is primarily using conducting motions basically to control participation and to a much lesser extent to obtain attending behavior. Acting motions are rather infrequent as is generally true; the only use is to emphasize, which in most classroom situations is more common than the use of pantomiming motions.

Since this teacher was working within a chalkboard-book lesson format, wieldings employed were rather limited to interaction with the chalk and the book. Wieldings, of course, would be more frequent and varied in situations in which the teacher uses paper, scissors, taperecorders, maps, projectors, crayon, paint pots, scientific equipment.

One warning must be interjected at this point. It would be unfortunate to characterize in a general way this teacher's performance based on this very limited teaching sample of less than two minutes. Teachers do vary in their physical activity from one episode to another.

That this is true can be understood by considering just how a cold can affect the personal motions of a teacher. The brushing of the nose might be a cold-associated motion that would not reappear in future episodes. Similarly if the teacher were using an overhead projector rather than the chalkboard, a different sequence of motions would result. If we sample episodes from a number of lessons, however, and find the same approximate numbers and kinds of bodily motion often appearing, we can begin to characterize the teacher's general patterns of motion.

When we looked at the classroom activity of a group of teachers whose behavior was analyzed in detail, we found that a single short episode taken from each of five lessons produced a rather consistent picture of the teacher's performance. Teachers do tend to have their own typical repertoire of motions upon which they draw again and again.

Chapter 3

# Teacher Motions and the Instructional Process

A teacher uses words, phrases, clauses, sentences to communicate instructional meanings in his classroom; likewise he uses gestures, nods, glances to communicate the same kinds of meanings. What are the kinds of meanings involved in instruction? What are the different ways in which teachers put these meanings together?

## HOW THE TEACHER FUNCTIONS

Until recently the classroom teacher has had relatively few frameworks for analyzing classroom meanings in a logical way. In the last ten years, however, descriptive frameworks have been projected that make it easier for a teacher to study his own activity patterns.

In one of the most useful patterns to be suggested, Arno Bellack categorizes the teaching act into four pedagogical functions—structuring, soliciting, responding, and reacting.[1] According to Bellack, a teacher *structures* when he sets the context for a classroom sequence—when he says things to open a discussion or to direct attention to an idea or a problem. The teacher is thus functioning as an initiator of pupil-teacher interaction as well as of pupil-pupil interaction. A teacher *solicits* when he says things designed to produce student responses. He is a solicitor when he asks questions, makes a request, or projects a command. A teacher *responds* in a classroom when he answers solicitation projected by others, i.e., when he answers student questions or

---

[1] Arno A. Bellack, Herbert M. Kliebard, Ronald T. Hyman, and Frank L. Smith, Jr., *The Language of the Classroom* (New York: Teachers College Press, 1966).

responds to a student command or request. The teacher *reacts* when he evaluates positively or negatively a student response; he reacts when he rewords a student response in order to clarify or elaborate upon it.

In short, what Bellack is suggesting is that the teacher communicates pedagogical meanings in these four different ways. Being able to function in these ways is the stock-in-trade of the teacher in the typical classroom situation.

The work of Bellack focuses primarily on verbal communication in the classroom; it has been centered on the way a teacher uses words to structure, solicit, respond, and react. Yet since these categories identify basic areas of teacher functioning, can they not be used to study physical as well as verbal motions in the classroom and to analyze the relationships between physical motions and verbal motions? The answer is "yes," for through a specific motion of the hand a teacher can structure; through a nod of the head a teacher can react or respond; through a waving of the fingers a teacher can solicit. The meanings a teacher is trying to communicate through structuring, soliciting, responding, and reacting can be communicated non-verbally.

Student teachers working within the Bellack framework have been able to look at video tapes of lessons and break these lessons down into small segments or "teaching moves." Although these moves may involve several motions, they serve only one pedagogical function or communicate only one kind of instructional meaning: they involve only soliciting, only structuring, only responding, or only reacting. In addition, student teachers have been able to identify within teaching moves both verbal and non-verbal motions or components.

Thus in looking at teaching as it occurs in today's classroom, we can say that what seems to be involved is the production of sequences of moves. For instance, a teacher may first make a move that structures, followed by one that solicits, followed by one that responds. Then the teacher may structure again, solicit again, and then react. Some of these moves may be totally verbal, some totally non-verbal; others may involve both verbal and non-verbal motions.

## HOW TEACHERS CARRY ON THE PEDAGOGICAL FUNCTIONS

How do teachers actually structure, solicit, respond, and react? To find an answer, we shall look at some of the motions, both verbal and non-verbal, that teachers use.

### Verbal Motions that Serve a Function

First, teachers structure, solicit, respond, and react through verbal statements. At times, they speak without perceptible body motion; in these instances communication is via the words and linguistic structures projected, the intonation of the words, the pauses, and the stresses. At other times, there is some bodily motion, but primary instructional meanings are communicated verbally.

Basically verbal maneuvers form the foundation of instruction. Only through the use of words can sophisticated, logical, and creative ideas be expressed. If we try to carry on a "conversation" with someone who does not speak our language, motions of hand and body produce only the simplest understanding. In the classroom this is equally true. The teacher may use a wave of the hand to communicate, "What do you think, John?" Yet, how can a teacher non-verbally ask: "If bluejays suddenly became extinct, what effect would that have on other organisms?" At this level of sophistication, faced with a discussion of a complicated if-then relationship, the teacher must use the verbal as his main means of communication.

Examples of verbal motions that can serve the structuring function are: "Today we are going to study the verb of being." "We will read the story silently during the next twenty minutes." "All right, that's all the time we have for the discussion of this story." Examples of verbal motions that serve the soliciting function are: "John, will you answer the first question on the board?" "Pay attention, John!" Examples of verbal motions that serve the responding function are: "No, you don't put the subject first." "I am not certain, John." "It is possible to explore that topic from that point of view." Examples of verbal motions that serve the reacting function are: "Very good, John! The subject is Mary." "That is partly right; at times in informal writing we do use the second form." "That is written very well, John."

### Non-verbal Motions that Serve a Function

Analysis of classroom interaction indicates that teachers also use physical motions to solicit, structure, respond, and react—actually to serve the pedagogical function. In such instances, teachers use no oral, linguistic counterpart or accompaniment. Their physical actions communicate instructional meaning.

Teachers have been observed structuring non-verbally. A teacher points to a reading assignment on the board. This action "says" that these pages will be taken next. Similarly a teacher may structure by placing a diagram on the board or by turning on a projector. These actions may be saying: "This is what we'll do next."

Many times teachers have been observed soliciting non-verbally. The following listing indicates some non-verbal, soliciting motions noted in classrooms and the meanings implied:

| Non-verbal solicitations | Meaning implied |
|---|---|
| Surveying group | Who's ready? |
| Raising hand | Would you please raise your hand? |
| Pointing with mike to a child | Begin the story. |
| Nodding at a child | Please answer. |
| Extending hand toward child in stop position | Wait just one minute; we'll take you next. |
| Motioning with hand in circular pattern | Turn around in your seat. |
| Holding up hand to group of children who are laughing | Stop laughing! |
| Placing finger to lips | Please be quiet! |
| Cupping ear with hand | Speak louder. |
| Pointing with index finger from one child to another | Do you want to answer Johnny's question? |

In each of these cases the non-verbal motion actually solicits; for this reason we say that the motion serves the pedagogical function of soliciting.

Teachers also have been observed responding completely in a non-verbal way. In one situation a child asked the teacher if he might leave the room. The teacher responded by pointing to the doorway, implying "Yes, you may." In another instance a child had raised his hand during a writing period, indicating he needed help. The teacher responded non-verbally by walking toward the child. Still another teacher's shrug of shoulders was a non-verbal response meaning: "I don't know."

Examples of non-verbal motions teachers use to react and the meanings implied are:

| Non-verbal reaction | Meaning implied |
|---|---|
| Handing the chalk to a child | Write the answer you gave on the board. |
| Clapping hands together | Wonderful! |
| Tilting head slightly | The answer is not entirely correct. |
| Writing word child gives on the easel | That's right. |
| Shaking head as he turns child's paper around | That's wrong. |

Even a cursory examination of the lists of meanings communicated

## Teacher Motions and the Instructional Process 29

by physical motions suggests the point previously made—that non-verbal motions are not used to communicate sophisticated meanings. The meanings are quite simple. Yet they are basic to the instructional process. The student learns "Yes, I am right," or "Ah, ha, he knows I'm not paying attention," or "I'm next," or "That's what I'm supposed to read." The observer in the classroom who focuses primarily on verbal interchange can totally miss these meanings; if that observer is a student teacher, he may conclude that this class is a good class; there are no discipline problems, for the senior teacher never reprimands. When that student teacher takes over and does not use the non-verbal devices so fundamental to good discipline in that classroom, he can learn the hard way that physical motion serves basic pedagogical purposes.

If we compare the actual number of individual body motions of the teacher to the actual number of individual verbal motions he makes, we find that non-verbal motions do occur more frequently than verbal motions. This evidence suggests the importance of the non-verbal in instruction. Yet, this does not indicate that non-verbal activity is more important than verbal; when the number of non-verbal motions used to serve a function (soliciting, structuring, etc.) is compared statistically to the number of verbal motions that serve a pedagogical function, we find that a far larger number of verbal motions serve a function than do non-verbal motions.

### *Physical Motions that Facilitate a Function*

Not all physical motions serve a function; some motions are not in themselves structuring, soliciting, responding, or reacting maneuvers. Rather, these bodily motions facilitate verbal and other non-verbal motions; and in this respect the motions reinforce, amplify, or modify what the words are saying or what other actions are communicating.

In the same way that physical motions can serve to structure, so they can support verbal motions that structure. The teacher may say:

| *Verbal Structuring* | *Supporting Physical Motion* |
|---|---|
| "I think that we are ready to go outside" ⟶ while ↗ | Looking around the classroom, |

or

| | |
|---|---|
| "We are going to read about *Pilgrims*" ⟶ while ↗ | Using emphasizing hand motion on the word Pilgrims. |

Physical motions can also support soliciting remarks. The teacher may ask:

| Verbal Soliciting | Supporting Physical Motion |
|---|---|
| "Do you have a loud dog?" ⟶ while ↗ | Leaning forward toward the child, |

or

| | |
|---|---|
| "Who knows something about the Mayflower?" ⟶ while ↗ | Moving head to the rhythmic flow of words, |

or

| | |
|---|---|
| "John, will you come to the board?" ⟶ while ↗ | Beckoning with the hand to the child. |

Similarly, teachers have been observed responding verbally, while using bodily motion to support their words. The teacher answers:

| Verbal Responding | Supporting Physical Motion |
|---|---|
| "Yes, you may go to the office." ⟶ while ↗ | Pointing toward the doorway, |

or

| | |
|---|---|
| "John, you may leave now." ⟶ while ↗ | Nodding his head at the child, |

or

| | |
|---|---|
| "Yes" in answer to a question ⟶ while ↗ | Nodding head, |

or

| | |
|---|---|
| "No" in answer to a question ⟶ while ↗ | Shaking his head. |

In like manner, the teacher uses physical actions to reinforce statements in which he reacts. He says:

| Verbal Reacting | Supporting Physical Motion |
|---|---|
| "Right, John." ⟶ while ⟶ | Writing John's answer on the easel, |

or

| | |
|---|---|
| "Excellent, Pete." ⟶ while ⟶ | Emphasizing words with hands, |

or

| | |
|---|---|
| "Yes, grasshoppers have antennae." ⟶ while ⟶ | Putting fingers to head to imitate a grasshopper. |

Finally, the teacher uses physical actions to facilitate other physical actions. For instance, before the teacher can react by writing John's answer on the easel, he has to pick up the felt pen from the desk, remove the top from it, straighten the paper on the easel, and place the top of the pen on its back. All these motions support his reaction to John.

The felt pen example explains in part why there are more physical motions than verbal motions in a classroom. Any one verbal act may require a sequence of physical motions to convey clearly the meanings intended. In this context non-verbal activity is a back-up support for the major verbal classroom activity.

### *Physical Motions that Do Not Relate to Teaching Functions*

One teacher was observed as she said, "She probably had quite a surprise. Don't you think?" As she made the remark, she was also

> removing her bangs from her face with a quick jerk of the head,
> feeling beads with both hands,
> moving the beads around her neck,
> feeling the beads with her thumb and index finger, and
> pulling on the beads.

It was obvious to the observers and it is obvious in retrospect that none of these physical motions is related to the instructional process going on in the classroom. The pulling on beads is not an attempt to structure, to solicit, to respond, or to react. It involves personal motions extraneous to the basic classroom functioning.

If the pedagogical functions are perceived as means through which the teacher attempts to order purposefully the classroom environment both verbally and non-verbally, then all physical motions of the personal variety cannot be considered as either serving or facilitating a pedagogical function. They can only be considered aspects of the classroom environment, which may or may not have a positive effect on the teaching. That such motions may well have a negative effect—a distracting effect—can be perceived from a second example, taken from an actual running account of teacher behavior. The teacher was observed

> clasping his hands,
> rubbing his hands together,
> clasping his hands again,
> placing hands under chin,
> placing "pinky" finger in mouth, and
> rubbing teeth with pinky.

During this time he said, "No, just Puzzle A and Puzzle D—Part I." The observer can validly ask: Did the teacher's "hand work" draw the students' attention away from the point under discussion? Most probably it did.

## TEACHING PATTERNS

When teaching is analyzed in terms of its components, it proves to be a highly complex system of verbal and non-verbal operations that interrelate and that often occur simultaneously. One way of looking at this system that has proved helpful to students of teaching is to eliminate from consideration all personal motions and then to study all the possible combinations of verbal and physical components that can occur. Knowing the possible combinations, a teacher can look at his own teaching to determine the kinds of patterns he tends to use. Five different patterns have been identified from actual classroom lessons.

### Teaching Pattern A: A Verbal/Non-verbal Pattern

We have found that teachers very commonly make statements that structure, solicit, respond, or react and at the same time make physical motions that tend to facilitate or support the words. For instance, a teacher may react by saying, "Good, you found the main point, John." At the same time he nods his head. The two motions—one verbal and one non-verbal—are components of a reacting move. The oral statement serves or carries on the pedagogical function of reacting to John; the physical motion facilitates or reinforces that statement.

Sometimes a verbal statement that forms the nucleus of a move has a string or a series of related physical motions that facilitate or support the words. For instance, the teacher who reacts by saying "Good, you found the main point, John," may not only nod his head but also (1) walk to the board, (2) pick up the chalk, (3) break the chalk in two, (4) put one piece down, (5) write John's answer on the board. In this case the move is more complex; it comprises a verbal motion and five non-verbal motions that support one pedagogical function—reacting.

A teaching pattern involving a verbal component and one or more physical motions that facilitate the pedagogical purpose under way at that point can be called Teaching Pattern A. We have found this pattern to be the most popular one among those teachers sampled in the background study; Table 2 gives the statistical detail and indicates that teaching has as a basic aspect the production of verbal–non-verbal

TABLE 2. TEACHING PATTERNS

| | |
|---|---|
| Pattern A: Verbal/Non-verbal | 60.5% |
| Pattern B: Verbal | 8.2% |
| Pattern C: Abortive | 0.1% |
| Pattern D: Non-verbal/Non-verbal | 10.2% |
| Pattern E: Non-verbal | 21.0% |

patterns. The diagram below schematically suggests what this teaching pattern may look like in a variety of moves.

*A Structuring Move—Pattern A*

| Verbal Component | Non-verbal Component |
|---|---|
| "Our emphasis today is on Japan." | Goes to board<br>Picks up pointer<br>Points to Japan on map |

*A Soliciting Move—Pattern A*

| Verbal Component | Non-verbal Component |
|---|---|
| "What is the capital of Japan?" | Surveys the class<br>Raises pointer<br>Points to child |

*A Responding Move—Pattern A*

| Verbal Component | Non-verbal Component |
|---|---|
| (answering a student question)<br>"Japan is a small country, but the people are highly industrious." | Moves hands together to emphasize |

*A Reacting Move—Pattern A*

| Verbal Component | Non-verbal Component |
|---|---|
| "I think you have it!" | Nodding head that is slightly cocked to side |

**Teaching Pattern B: A Verbal Pattern**

An obvious pattern of motion in the classroom involves only verbal motion. The teacher makes a statement in which he may react or respond, solicit or structure, but he does this without perceptible movement of his body. An example of a Teaching Pattern B is the instance in which the teacher reacts only with, "Excellent, Sue!"

Table 2 gives the statistical data on how teachers in the sample group used this pattern. In summary, it would be safe to say that the use of this pattern in no way approaches the popularity of Pattern A; teachers tend not to employ a state of complete motionlessness as an accompaniment to their words.

### Teaching Pattern C: An Abortive Pattern

Several instances of teacher behavior have been noted on video tape in which non-verbal activity takes place but in which the verbal component that normally should result never comes to pass. In a sense the physical motion is abortive.

One teacher was observed lowering his head and scanning the page of a book held in his hand to search for the next question. Yet because of some other happening in the room or a change of mind, he did not ask the next question in the sequence.

Another teacher tended to follow a pattern of pointing to a word on a chart, saying the word, pointing to a child to give the antonym, pointing to next word on the chart, saying that word, pointing to another child, etc. After the last word, momentarily not realizing it was the last, she turned to the chart, pointed to the chart, and then turned away. Her final motions were abortive.

Table 2 indicates that abortive patterns are very rare. When the teachers in the sample group began a move, they almost always carried it out completely.

### Teaching Pattern D: A Non-verbal/Non-verbal Pattern

Another teaching pattern observed in classroom interaction appears in the following example: Steve answers a question correctly. As a means of pedagogically reacting to Steve's answer, the teacher nods his head—a non-verbal device that functions without words. Then the teacher turns to the board, raises his hand to write, and records the answer on the board.

What is happening in this example? The teacher is using a physical motion to serve the reacting function; then he uses a series of other physical motions to reinforce the initial physical motions. In this case both the basic operation and the supporting actions within the move are non-verbal. As Table 2 indicates, the case study teachers used this pattern about as frequently as they used Pattern B, but much less frequently than they used Pattern A.

### Teaching Pattern E: A Non-verbal Pattern

Teachers also have a fifth pattern in their repertoire of classroom moves. Quite simply, they make a single physical motion that serves or carries out a pedagogical function; with one motion, they structure, solicit, respond, or react; and they say nothing. The teacher who responds to a student request to leave the room by shaking his head is applying this pattern as is the teacher who solicits student attention by pointing his finger. As Table 2 indicates, the teachers who participated in the current study used this pattern more frequently than they used Patterns B and D.

## TEACHING CHAINS

In *The Language of the Classroom,* Arno Bellack reports results of an investigation into the language behavior of teachers. According to his study, done at the secondary level, teachers tend to function pedagogically primarily as solicitors, secondly as reactors, and thirdly as structurers. Although teachers do use statements in response, they respond much less frequently than they carry on other classroom functions.

Although the Bellack study did not involve an analysis of non-verbal behavior of teachers, his results were replicated in the current study, in which verbal and non-verbal components of teacher moves were considered. Once again the teachers in the sample group proved to be primarily solicitors and secondly reactors.

Study of the actual video tapes of the teachers suggests that teachers seem to use these moves in a rather repetitive, chainlike fashion. They structure-solicit-react, solicit-react, solicit-react . . . in almost endless chains. Occasionally a student interjects a question to which the teacher responds, and this breaks the chain. Then too, of course, the teacher periodically restructures and begins another chain.

Couple to the chainlike use of soliciting-reacting sequences the predominant use of Teaching Pattern A (verbal/non-verbal), and we have a rather solid description of what teaching is all about in the ordinary situation. This description gives rise to the question: "How can the teacher break the repetitive sequence so typical of average teaching?" or "How can he add variety to his motions?"

## A COMPREHENSIVE SYSTEM FOR LOOKING AT MOTION

How does the system operate? Although Figure 1 illustrates the overall design of the system for analysis, a more detailed explanation is needed for the teacher who is interested in studying his own teaching. Such an explanation is given in this section, using an actual teaching episode.

### The Framework

Let us examine a very brief teaching episode that occurred in a fourth grade classroom in terms of the concepts just discussed. To do so, we can identify and look at the teaching moves to determine whether they serve the structuring, soliciting, responding, or reacting function. Then each of the moves must be examined to determine of what kind of motions they are composed—whether they contain:

1. a verbal motion that serves the pedagogical function (V/S), or
2. a non-verbal motion that serves the pedagogical function (NV/S), and also
3. non-verbal motions that facilitate or support another motion (NV/F), and
4. non-verbal motions that are unrelated to the teaching process (P).

Next the different combination of verbal and non-verbal motions composing a move must be examined to determine the teaching patterns involved. In addition, we can look at the kinds of physical motions to determine if they are either instructional or personal. If physical motions are instructional, we can determine if each is conducting, acting, or wielding.

### The Episode

In the following sequence, the teacher's words are in quotation marks in the left-hand column, students' comments are in parentheses in the middle column, the physical motions of the teacher are in the right-hand column, and the teacher's pedagogical moves are noted numerically in sequential order.

1. "Right!"            Looks back down at chart
                                        Turns chart so next child can see
                                        Points to next word on chart
                                2. Looks up at next child

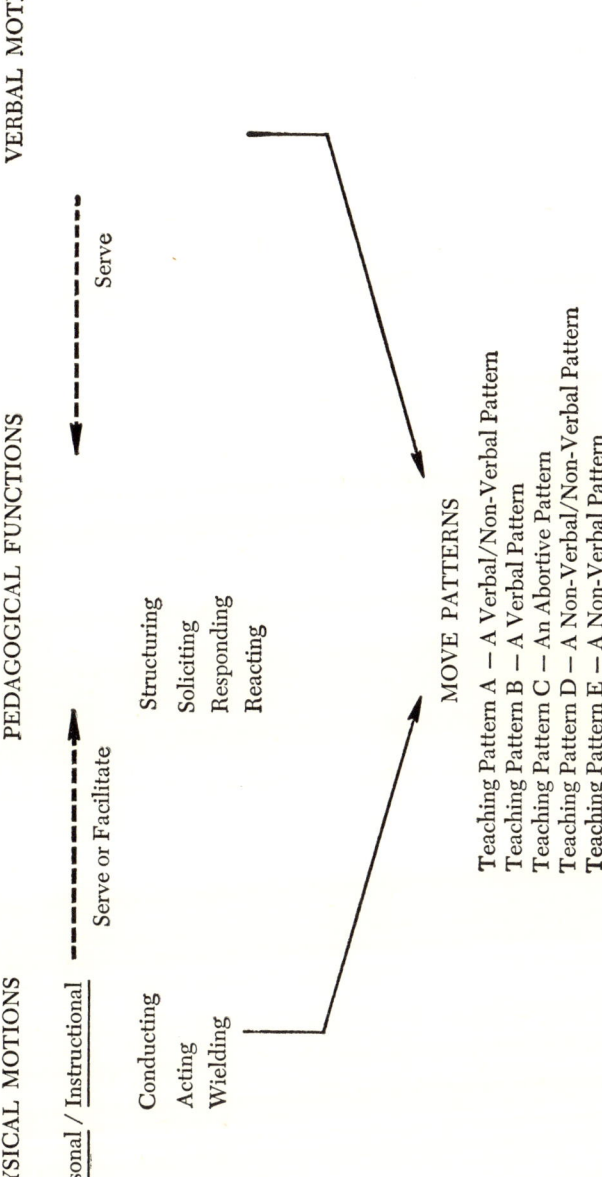

Figure 1. The System for Analysis.

38   THE TEACHER MOVES

(Child says: "kwit")

3. "Right!"                  Looks back down at the chart
                                Turns chart so that next child can see
                  4. Looks up at child

(Child says: "kwiz")

5. "Very good"          6. Looks back down at chart to direct child's attention to next word

(Child calls out: "there wasn't one for Leslie")

                           Lowers chart
                           Turns chart to face herself in reading position
                           Scans chart with small head motions
                           Looks up at Leslie

7. "Well, she can have the first one from the next one."

                         Scratches chin
                         Looks down at chart

8. "O.K., 'kw' is what sound?"      Looks up at children in group

                  9. Surveys the group in a way that asks: "Who would like to answer?"

(Children raise hands.)

### *Looking at the Episode*

During this brief teaching sequence, the teacher actually made nine different pedagogical moves. The first move is a verbal *reacting* one, in which the teacher is evaluating or rating a child's previous answer with a single word "Right!" The second move has a major non-verbal component. When the teacher looks up at the next child, she is communicating: "Sally, you take the next question." This move is a *soliciting* one, and in order to make that solicitation, the teacher makes three additional physical motions: she looks down at the chart, turns the chart so the next child can see, and points to the next word on the chart. For this reason, these three motions are part of that solicitation; they facilitate or support the non-verbal motion.

The third move again has a single component, the word "Right!" The teacher is *reacting*, and, of course, in a verbal way. The fourth move basically repeats the second. The teacher *solicits* non-verbally by looking at the child whom she wants to respond. Her looking back down at the chart and turning the chart so that the child can see support the non-verbal solicitation and, therefore, are components of that move.

As her fifth move the teacher *reacts* with her words, "Very good." The teacher then begins to *solicit;* in her sixth move she looks down at the chart to focus on the next word, but finding none she aborts that move and responds to the child's outburst with a *responding* move —"Well, she can have the first one from the next one." As she makes this seventh move in the sequence, she makes a whole series of non-verbal motions from lowering the chart to looking at Leslie to scratching her chin. The scratching is a non-verbal motion that does not relate to the instructional functioning; it is personal or self-adjusting. But the other non-verbal motions support her verbal response.

The eighth move in the sequence is a verbal *solicitation*, "O.K., 'kw' is what sound?" It is supported by two physical motions, her looking down at the chart and her looking up at the children. The final move in the series is a non-verbal *solicitation,* in which she surveys her class in typical teacher fashion that means: "Who would like to answer?"

What are the patterns this teacher employs? In most of the cases just given the patterns are obvious:

    Move 1: Pattern B: verbal
    Move 2: Pattern D: non-verbal/non-verbal
    Move 3: Pattern B: verbal
    Move 4: Pattern D: non-verbal/non-verbal
    Move 5: Pattern B: verbal
    Move 6: Pattern C: abortive
    Move 7: Pattern A: verbal/non-verbal
    Move 8: Pattern A: verbal/non-verbal
    Move 9: Pattern E: non-verbal

Now look at the teaching chains—the sequence of moves the teacher uses:

    Move 1: Reacting
    Move 2: Soliciting
    Move 3: Reacting
    Move 4: Soliciting
    Move 5: Reacting
    Move 6: Soliciting
    Move 7: Responding
    Move 8: Soliciting
    Move 9: Soliciting

TABLE 3. AN ANALYSIS OF A TEACHING EPISODE.

| Move # | Type Move | Verbal Component Serves | Non-verbal Component Serves* | Non-verbal Component(s) Facilitates* | Pattern | Personal |
|---|---|---|---|---|---|---|
| 1. | 4 Reacting | V/S | | | B | |
| 2. | 2 Soliciting | | NV/S 1.1 | 1.1 1.1 1.1 | D | |
| 3. | 4 Reacting | V/S | | | B | |
| 4. | 2 Soliciting | | NV/S 1.1 | 1.1 1.1 | D | |
| 5. | 4 Reacting | V/S | | | B | |
| 6. | 2 Soliciting | does not serve— move aborted | | 1.1 | C | |
| 7. | 3 Responding | V/S | | 3.3 3.3 3.2 **1.1** | A | P |
| 8. | 2 Soliciting | V/S | | 1.1 1.1 | A | |
| 9. | 2 Soliciting | | NV/S 1.1 | | E | |

* Non-verbal motions are classified according to the scheme developed above, Chapter 2. (Conducting 1.0, Acting 2.0, Wielding 3.0.)

A cursory analysis of the kinds of physical motions employed during the episode indicates that of the sixteen motions only one is personal or self-adjusting; all the others are instructional. Using the techniques outlined in Chapter 2, we see that most of the instructional motions can be considered "conducting" in order to "control participation." Only when the teacher lowers the chart, turns it to face herself, and scans it with small head motions is she "wielding." There are no "acting" motions noted during the episode. This information is summarized in Table 3.

What are the most noteworthy aspects of this teaching episode? Without a doubt, the most striking aspect is the repetitive use of reacting-soliciting-reacting moves that typifies many discussion lessons; this teacher is employing the traditional chaining of question-answer-reinforcement, question-answer-reinforcement, question-answer-reinforcement as the major structure for the lesson. Second, this teacher does employ a full range of teaching patterns, even patterns not very often used in classrooms; she uses non-verbal motions to carry on the pedagogical functioning as well as to support her verbal and even other non-verbal activities. Third, the teacher's non-verbal motions are the common ones associated with conducting—she points, she looks up to control participation—and like many teachers she does not use motion to illustrate, to emphasize, or to role play. The number of personal motions she uses is limited.

# Chapter 4

# *Teacher Motions and Teaching Style*

What can we learn about teaching style from focusing on the way a teacher moves in the classroom? When we looked at the performances of the five teachers whose classroom behavior we studied in detail, we discovered basic differences that indicate dimensions of teacher style relevant to all teaching. Some differences were of a quantitative nature; others were more qualitative.

Among the case study teachers, quantitative differences were found in:

1. the total number of motions performed by teachers in comparable units of time;
2. the verbal/non-verbal orientation of the teachers;
3. the physical motions that predominate in teacher performances;
4. the moves that predominate in their performance;
5. the number of physical motions used to serve each pedagogical function, e.g., to structure, to solicit, to respond, to react;
6. the patterns used; and
7. the internal variance of their performances.

Qualitative differences were found in:

1. the specific kinds of personal hand gestures and body motions that predominate;
2. the specific kinds of instructional gestures and body motions that predominate; and
3. the speech patterns of the teachers—the actual words and speech characteristics that predominate.

## DIMENSIONS OF TEACHING STYLE

In this section we shall describe non-verbal dimensions that seem to be integral aspects of a teacher's style.

### Activity

A group of student teachers was sent into a series of classrooms with the assignment: "Observe the amount of motion the teachers use." Their informal conclusion that *teachers can be placed on an activity continuum* was verified by the performances of the five teachers whose behavior has been studied in a more systematic way.

Teachers do differ from one another in the total number of motions —both verbal and non-verbal—they carry out during a similar period of time. Some teachers appear to be human dynamos in a continual state of activity. They walk here and there; they gesture, and they manipulate things around them; one word follows another in rapid succession. In contrast are the more passive teachers, whose motions are limited in number. Their bodies tend to remain still, and they do not talk to such a great extent. Of course, too, there are teachers who fall somewhere between the two extremes. In short, a teacher's "activity quotient" can be plotted on a continuum ranging from high activity through average activity to low activity.

That the spread within the activity continuum is extremely broad can be noted by considering just how the five teachers in the sample group differ along this dimension. In ten minutes of teaching (composed of five two-minute segments, each withdrawn from a different lesson), one teacher performed 829 distinct verbal and non-verbal motions whereas another teacher performed only 617 motions—a difference of more than 200 motions.

These same broad differences in amount of activity also appear when verbal and non-verbal components of total activity are considered separately. The number of physical motions used by the teachers ranged from a high of 671 for one teacher to a low of 403 for another —a difference of more than 250 motions. The number of verbal motions ranged from a high of 158 for one teacher to a low of 94 for a second teacher—a difference of more than fifty motions. (See Appendix, Table A-2.)

### Verbal/Non-verbal Orientation

Our research evidence seems to indicate that, when the number of verbal motions used by a teacher is compared to the number of distinct non-verbal motions employed during the same period, the latter far exceeds the former. As a matter of fact, in the group of teachers studied systematically as a foundation for this book, 81.6% of the motions were non-verbal, 18.4% were verbal.

Looking at individual teacher behavior, however, we have found that some teachers have a greater orientation toward non-verbal communication than other teachers; similarly some teachers have a greater orientation toward verbal communication. That this is so is readily picked up in informal classroom observations. Some teachers forever seem to be beckoning and nodding and walking; they are the doers. Other teachers may move less and talk more; they are the speakers.

Another kind of evidence that can be used to determine the verbal/non-verbal orientation of a teacher is the number of verbal motions he uses to carry on or serve one of the fundamental pedagogical functions compared with the number of non-verbal motions he uses to serve these functions. Among the teachers sampled, verbal motions were used much more often to carry on pedagogical functions than were non-verbal motions; non-verbal motions generally were used to support verbal motions. Yet some teachers still tended to fall above average in the number of non-verbal motions they used pedagogically. These teachers have a greater non-verbal orientation in their communication than other practitioners. (See Appendix, Tables A-4 and A-5.)

The result is a continuum that is a second dimension of teaching style—a verbal/non-verbal continuum along which teacher performance can be mapped.

### *Conducting-Acting-Wielding Ratios*

Teachers are primarily conductors, secondly wielders, and thirdly actors if we consider the total number of conducting motions, wielding motions, and acting motions performed. And yet if we look at each teacher's ratio of conductings-actings-wieldings, we find that this ratio is a distinctive aspect of his style. If the average conducting-acting-wielding ratio of a group of teachers is 62.5 : 8.8 : 28.7, and if an individual teacher's ratio is 81.4 : 9.0 : 9.6, one unique aspect of this teacher's style is immediately apparent—his greater use of conducting and his lesser use of wielding than is typical of other teachers in the group.

Similar kinds of ratios for a teacher can be projected for components of conducting (controlling participation : obtaining attending behavior), for components of acting (emphasizing : illustrating : role playing), and for components of wielding (direct : indirect : instrumental).

Again these ratios, when compared with average ratios of a larger group of teachers, indicate unique dimensions of teaching style.

From this type of information we can make generalizations about a teacher's unique style, e.g., his distinctive use of role playing, his relatively high use of motions that obtain attending behavior, or his relatively small use of reading motions—indirect wieldings.

### Instructional-Personal Ratio

Still another dimension of teaching style is the number of personal bodily motions compared to the number of instructional bodily motions a teacher employs. When undergraduate education students focused their classroom observation on the comparative use of instructional and personal motions, they reacted with such realistic comments as: "He seemed to scratch, fiddle, or twist incessantly," or "She seemed to use motion in an almost deliberate way; every motion counted," or "She must have pushed up her glasses at least once every three minutes." It is obvious to the classroom observer that teachers do differ in their instructional-personal ratios.

On the other hand, among the five teachers in the case study group, only minor differences in amount of personal motions were perceived. This was probably due to the teachers' experience and their higher level of showmanship acquired through the long observation of their behavior in a demonstration school setting. (See Appendix, Table A-2.)

### Structuring-Soliciting-Responding-Reacting Ratio

Although teachers tend to use more soliciting and reacting moves than they do structuring and responding moves, they differ in the emphasis they place on each type of pedagogical functioning. Some tend to structure more than is typical, whereas others use more responding moves; some tend to solicit more than is typical, whereas others use more reacting moves. As a result, the structuring-soliciting-responding-reacting ratio tells us something about the unique aspects of a teacher's style.

For example, among our five case study teachers, the overall structuring-soliciting-responding-reacting ratio is 7.6 : 65.5 : 2.6 : 24.3. One teacher's ratio is 1.2 : 63.7 : 1.8 : 33.3. Obviously this teacher has her classroom activities organized in such a way that she almost never needs to structure or to respond either verbally or non-verbally. (See Appendix, Table A-6.)

Another facet of this dimension is whether the teacher uses verbal or non-verbal means to carry out each of the four pedagogical functions.

Of course, as has already been suggested, teachers typically use verbal devices to perform the functions; yet some teachers tend to employ a higher than average proportion of non-verbal devices in carrying out certain functions. For example, one teacher may use a higher than average proportion of non-verbal motions to react; whereas a second teacher may use a lower than average proportion of non-verbal motions to do the same job. Likewise, another teacher may tend to solicit almost totally at the verbal level and rarely, if ever, use non-verbal motions to carry on this particular pedagogical function. (See Appendix, Tables A-7 and A-8.)

### *Teaching Pattern Tendencies*

The way in which a teacher differs from the average in use of teaching patterns is still another dimension of his style. In the group of teachers studied, we found a preferential use of teaching Pattern A. The largest percentage of moves involved a verbal statement supported by one or more non-verbal motions. There was, however, some variation among the teachers in preferential use of move patterns, one using a higher number of completely non-verbal patterns, a second using very few patterns involving a major non-verbal component with other non-verbal motions supporting it, a third running low on number of Pattern A's employed. Such tendencies are an important aspect of style. (See Appendix, Table A-9.)

### *Internal Variance*

One teacher uses an extreme amount of physical motion during one or two lessons, very little during one or two others. A second teacher uses many conducting motions on a number of occasions, very few during other lessons. A third teacher makes many reacting moves on several occasions, very few during other lessons. We can say that such teachers vary within themselves in the use of motion. Their performances are internally inconsistent; and, therefore, when their classroom behavior is studied statistically, high variance scores result.

By contrast a teacher uses a high proportion of acting motions in almost every context. Another teacher has a preference for Move Pattern D, which shows up in almost every lesson. Still another teacher tends to employ a high proportion of responding moves, a tendency that is noted over and over again. These teachers do not vary to any great extent in their use of these kinds of motion. Their performances are internally consistent; and when their classroom behavior is studied statistically, relatively low variance scores result.

Whether a teacher's performance is internally consistent is a dimension of that teacher's style. That this is so can be easily seen by looking at extreme cases. The first case is the teacher who uses about the same number and kinds of all motions, moves, and patterns. Each lesson tends to be just about the same with no highs nor lows to break the sameness. In such a case the repetitiveness is a key aspect of the teacher's style. The second teacher goes to the opposite extreme; in each lesson, he uses different amounts and kinds of patterns, motions, and moves. There is no sameness in his approach; and in this case the high variance may be the most unique facet of his style.

### Instructional Repertoire

If we go into a classroom to observe a teacher for an extended period of time, it becomes obvious that the teacher's repertoire of instructional gestures, facial expressions, and bodily activity is unique. This repertoire may contain a basic nucleus of specific motions that typify his performance and a cluster of specific motions that reappear to a lesser extent. For example, one teacher may have in his basic repertoire: (1) pointing to identify who will recite, (2) nodding to approve of a student response, (3) walking toward a child as the child recites, (4) picking up a book, (5) looking down at the book, and (6) moving his index finger up and down to emphasize important words. His secondary repertoire includes: (1) waving at a misbehaving student, (2) running his finger under important words written on the board, and (3) flicking the lights on and off for attention. Of course, this teacher does use other specific motions, but less frequently.

To see that the teacher's repertoire of motions is an aspect of his style, let us look at the repertoire of a second teacher. Motions in his basic repertoire are: (1) shaking head at misbehaving student, (2) nodding to identify who will recite, (3) smiling in approval at a student's response, (4) frowning in disapproval, (5) turning on overhead projector, and (6) pointing with a stick at image projected. His secondary repertoire includes: (1) walking while talking, (2) using his forefingers to illustrate, and (3) pointing with pencil in hand to focus attention.

How do these two teachers differ? A rapid comparison of their basic and secondary repertoires indicates that they employ rather different motions to communicate instructional meanings. Each has a style uniquely his own.

### Personal Repertoire

Not only does a teacher have an instructional repertoire; he also has a personal repertoire of specific motions that recur in his teaching.

Again there are specific motions that predominate and are part of the teacher's style; there are specific motions that appear to a lesser extent. In the basic repertoire, of course, are the mannerisms that, because of their constant repetitive use, may detract. In addition, there are the bodily motions that tend to recur because of some continuing fundamental physical characteristic of the teacher: the wearing of glasses, necklaces, tight collars, loose sweaters.

Again let us compare two teachers. The first teacher has this basic repertoire: (1) pushes up his glasses, (2) rubs his nose, (3) loosens his collar, (4) leans against the desk, and (5) props up one foot on a chair. In his secondary repertoire he (1) holds his hand under his chin, (2) taps fingers (as a nervous gesture) on the desk, and (3) takes off and puts on glasses.

The second teacher has within his basic repertoire: (1) scratching his head, (2) pulling on his ear lobe, (3) balancing on the back of his chair with feet on seat, (4) twisting a pencil in his hand, and (5) fiddling with his tie clasp. In his secondary repertoire are: (1) tossing up and catching a piece of chalk, and (2) holding hand to mouth as he clears throat.

Even a brief examination of the two teachers' recurring personal motions indicates that their performances in the classroom would appear rather different to an observer. Each is employing specific bodily motions that are integral aspects of his teaching style.

### Verbal Repertoire

As we have studied the video-tapes of classroom episodes and as we have amassed descriptions of teaching from observations made by teachers-in-training, it has become more and more evident that teachers not only have non-verbal repertoires but verbal repertoires—words, phrases, sentences, clauses that they repeatedly use, and characteristic ways of speaking. For instance, a facet of one teacher's verbal repertoire is the phrase, "Very good," which the teacher uses after a student's response; similarly another teacher tends to say, "That's right," whereas a third teacher generally reacts with a succinct, "Yes." In order to structure one teacher usually begins with, "And now we will look at . . .";  a second teacher tends to say, "The first thing we will do . . ."; whereas a third teacher remarks, "Let's begin by . . . ." In projecting questions, a teacher habitually asks, "Can anyone tell me . . .?" Another teacher's technique is to ask "Who can tell me . . .?" Still another teacher solicits with the words "Raise your hand if you know . . . ." These typical ways of organizing words are part of their verbal repertoires.

From personal experience we know that a teacher does have a

unique verbal repertoire. One of the writers taught at the junior high school level. When she began her teaching, she wondered how to refer to her students—"kids" is not very professional, and junior high young people react negatively to being called "children" or "boys and girls." She decided to say "people." "Now, people" she would say to gain attention. One day a boy in the class approached her: "Do you know, Miss Grant, that you have said people 127 times during the last month?" He had kept a tally of one major facet of the teacher's verbal repertoire.

There are other characteristics of speech that are part of a teacher's unique style. They include:

1. *Noise:* the "uh's" a teacher may have a tendency to inject between words. In a sense this is comparable to static heard on broadcasts.
2. *Juncture:* the pauses or moments of silence that a teacher may have a tendency to inject before important words, between sentences, even within words. In many instances the pause in spoken English is equivalent to punctuation in written English.
3. *Stress:* the oral emphasis a teacher may place on words, depending on their location in the sentence or on their importance.
4. *Tone:* the emotional level of speaking—e.g., excited, bored, unhappy, decisive, indecisive, sweet, gentle, pleasing, harsh.
5. *Speed:* the rate of speaking—fast, moderate, slow.
6. *Syntax:* the typical sentence patterns a teacher employs, the simplicity or complexity of his sentences.

## USING THE DIMENSIONS: CASE STUDIES OF TEACHING STYLE

How do the five teachers whose behavior we have studied in detail vary within these non-verbal dimensions of teaching style? This section projects a composite picture of each teacher's key characteristics in an attempt to show how vastly different basically experienced teachers can be and to indicate the range of options available to the teacher. For each teacher both qualitative and quantitative aspects of his performance are considered.

### *Mrs. Cynthia Walker: Grade 1*[1]

Mrs. Walker's basic non-verbal instructional motions are: (1) using index finger to emphasize, (2) writing down child's answer, (3) walking across front of class, (4) walking toward class, and (5) leaning

---
[1] The names of the teachers are fictitious.

toward child or children who should respond. Her secondary non-verbal repertoire includes: (1) tapping on paper or desk to get attention, (2) pointing to draw attention to an object, (3) turning and focusing her attention on a child, (4) moving hands in a way that means "everyone recite," (5) holding up hand when she wants children to raise hands, and (6) walking among group members.

These repertoires indicate that Mrs. Walker is a "walker," one who typically likes to walk around the classroom. She usually leans toward children rather than pointing or nodding to indicate who should recite. She also uses non-verbal motion to get the class to recite in unison and to overcome the pattern of having children call out the answer.

Her basic personal non-verbal repertoire includes: (1) making dance motions with feet, (2) twiddling chalk, (3) rolling chalk in hands, (4) feeling chalk with index finger and thumb, (5) removing bangs from forehead with quick jerk of head, and (6) feeling beads around neck and moving them from side to side. Her secondary personal non-verbal repertoire includes: (1) scratching nose, (2) placing elbow on knee when sitting, and (3) tapping chin.

A comparison of this teacher's personal and instructional repertoires suggests relationships. Mrs. Walker walks a great deal; and as she does, she moves her feet in a quick, interesting, personal pattern that is typically her own. The technician, who filmed her, was so taken by her movement that he remarked "Look at that footwork!" Also Mrs. Walker is a recorder; she likes to put students' answers on the board or easel. As a result she often has chalk in her hand, and tends to "play" with it.

Mrs. Walker has words that she tends to repeat. Her basic verbal repertoire includes: (1) reacting to students' answers with "All right" and "Good"; (2) soliciting by calling the name of student; and (3) using "You" in giving class directions. Her secondary verbal repertoire includes: (1) beginning directions with "Let's . . ."; (2) calling students "Boys and girls"; (3) saying "Raise your hand if you can think . . ." to prevent calling out; and (4) questioning "Can you think . . . ."

Mrs. Walker pauses rather than making "uh" noises between words. She tends to pause between sentences, before important words, and after asking a question to allow children to think. In this respect, she uses silence as a teaching device. She enunciates clearly and precisely, has a pleasing voice, and talks at a moderate pace. Her sentences are short, simple, and grammatically clear.

In many respects Mrs. Walker is the typical teacher in the group. First, when we consider her performance by looking at how many motions she uses, we find that she is *very close to average* in her activity—the total number of motions, the number of physical motions, and the number of verbal motions she makes. Likewise her structuring-soliciting-responding-reacting ratio is amazingly close to the average for the case study teachers.

Mrs. Walker shows no decided verbal or non-verbal orientation. The proportion of verbal and non-verbal motions she employs to serve a function is about average as is her use of Patterns A, B, C, D, and E. In only one respect is she more verbally than non-verbally inclined; she tends to react verbally rather than non-verbally.

Looking at the way Mrs. Walker uses conducting, acting, and wielding motions, we find her conducting-acting-wielding ratio is again close to average. The only distinctive feature of her performance is the kinds of conducting motions she makes. Mrs. Walker uses a higher per cent of motions to obtain attending behavior and thus a lower per cent of motions to control participation than is typical among the case study teachers. There is a relationship between this characteristic and aspects of her verbal/non-verbal repertoires. Recall that this teacher also tended to repeat such verbal motions as "Raise your hands if . . .," and such non-verbal motions as holding up her hand to indicate to a child to raise his hand—motions that have a disciplining implication.

Cynthia Walker's performance is distinctive in two ways. First, she uses more personal motions than is typical among the case study teachers. Second, her performance is less varied. Of all the case study teachers, she is the most consistent in the total number of motions she makes; she used about the same number of motions in each of her two-minute episodes studied. This generalization holds true for her total number of (1) verbal motions, (2) non-verbal motions, (3) instructional motions, (4) conducting and acting motions, (5) non-verbal and verbal motions used to serve a pedagogical function, and (6) Patterns A, B, C, D, and E. Her behavior thus is more constant and predictable from one lesson to the next and even within the same lesson than is that of the other teachers in her comparison group.

For the teacher or teacher-in-training, we raise some fundamental questions to be considered:

1. This teacher had to use many motions associated with disciplining. Is there anything about her style that might have contributed to this?
2. Would the teacher's high use of personal motions distract from her teaching?

3. What other non-verbal devices could she use to emphasize?
4. What additional devices could she use to get the attention of the class?
5. How can she vary her verbal reactions?
6. What are the advantages or disadvantages of performing in a less varied way?

**Mrs. Linda Higgins: Grade 2**

Mrs. Higgins' basic non-verbal instructional repertoire is: (1) touching child, (2) leaning over child, (3) putting arm around child, (4) exercising before lesson with the children to the rhythm of a free verse, (5) writing on board, (6) looking over or surveying the class before calling on a student, and (7) nodding at child. Her secondary non-verbal instructional repertoire is: (1) cocking head in a questioning way after she has asked a question, (2) holding chalk in hand, and (3) sitting on chair in front of children squatting on rug.

Her basic personal repertoire includes: (1) pushing bangs from forehead, (2) touching glasses, (3) stroking hair, and (4) scratching head. Her secondary personal repertoire includes: (1) clasping hands, (2) dropping hands to side, (3) placing hands behind back, (4) placing hand on book, and (5) playing with ring.

This teacher has certain features in her typical performance not found to the same extent in the repertoires of other case study teachers: exercising before the class, sitting before a rug, and maintaining physical contact with her children. Typically before a lesson Mrs. Higgins faces her class, raises her arms upward, and then slowly moves them downward with an undulating rhythm as she recites, "Stretch them high to the sky; float them down to the ground." The children participate in the action, which is repeated several times before the students get back into their seats. A second feature is a unique way of seating herself. She moves a low chair to a position immediately in front of a bright scatter rug thrown on the floor. She motions to one child to take a seat to her right, motions to a second to take a seat to her left, and motions to the others to sit on the rug. And from that position she instructs. A third feature of her non-verbal performance, which is most striking to an observer, is the physical contact she maintains with her students. She circulates physically in the classroom, leaning over a child and putting her arm around him. Another child may take her hand and move with her around the room, or she may touch a child on his back as a way of saying "Good."

Mrs. Higgins' basic verbal repertoire includes: (1) to get silence, "Sh-h-h"; (2) to react, "Very good"; (3) to reprimand, "Excuse me!";

and (4) for amenities, "Please." Her secondary verbal repertoire includes: (1) to call on student, says his name; (2) to react, "Good, thank you"; and (3) to solicit, "will you call on the next person?"

Aspects of her speech that are distinctive are:

1. *Noise:* such sounds as "ah-h-h-h," "oow-w-w-w, whow" noted.
2. *Juncture:* typically found between child's name and directive, as in "Calvin . . . sit right over here!" and "Peggy and Kathy . . . would you please come up front?"
3. *Stress:* emphasis on important words.
4. *Tone:* emotive, often with excitement in voice and yet rather humble and gentle.
5. *Speed:* moderate.
6. *Syntax:* short sentences.

From the statistical data we have about Mrs. Higgins, we know that of all the case study teachers she was the least active; the total number of actions both physical and verbal that she used during ten minutes of teaching was 528 as compared to a median number of 617. This same lower-level activity also shows up when we look at the number of physical motions she made; again she was the least active among the sample teachers. Only in her use of verbal motions is she above average, which indicates a verbal rather than non-verbal orientation in her teaching. She employs a higher than average number of verbal motions to serve a pedagogical function and, of course, a lower than average number of non-verbal motions to serve a function—again suggesting a verbal orientation. Mrs. Higgins' use of the five move patterns confirms this hypothesis. Her use of Pattern E (a single non-verbal motion) is the lowest of all the teachers.

Mrs. Higgins' conducting-acting-wielding ratio is 81.4 : 9.0 : 9.6, compared to an average ratio of 62.5 : 8.8 : 28.7. Obviously she is more a conductor and less a wielder than the other teachers. In addition, she is unique in her use of acting motions. She is the only one who makes pantomiming motions and the only one who uses acting motions to serve a pedagogical function.

Looking at Mrs. Higgins' structuring-soliciting-responding-reacting ratio, we find that this is one dimension in which she is rather close to the average for her group, her ratio being 7.5 : 62.1 : 1.1 : 29.3, compared to the mean ratio of 7.6 : 65.5 : 2.6 : 24.3. It is only as we focus on the non-verbal motions that serve these functions that any definitive differences appear. There we find that when Mrs. Higgins makes motions that react, she has a higher tendency to do so non-verbally than is typical among the case study teachers. Likewise, when she makes motions that solicit, she has a lower tendency to use non-verbal means than is typical.

Turning to the final dimension of teacher style—internal variance—we discover that Mrs. Higgins' overall performance tends to be rather similar in the number of motions made from one lesson to the next. She is consistent in (1) the total number of motions, (2) the proportion of verbal and non-verbal motions, (3) her conducting-acting-wielding ratio, (4) her non-verbal motions that serve and facilitate pedagogical functions, and (5) her use of Patterns A, B, C, D, and E. Actually, the data show that Mrs. Higgins' teaching is less varied than Mrs. Walker's.

For the teacher or teacher-in-training, we raise these questions:

1. Should we as teachers make physical contact with our students as Mrs. Higgins does?
2. This teacher is more verbally oriented than the others. What advantages does this have? What disadvantages does this have?
3. This teacher is least active. What advantages and disadvantages does this have?
4. Mrs. Higgins uses noise. Give a practical example to show when noise would be desirable in instruction, undesirable in instruction.

### *Miss Beverly Straton: Grade 3*

Miss Straton's basic non-verbal instructional repertoire is: (1) looking over class or surveying before calling on students, (2) nodding throughout a child's recitation, (3) nodding after a child's recitation, and (4) cocking head in a questioning way. Her secondary non-verbal instructional repertoire includes: (1) pointing to a child to recite, (2) picking up chart, (3) pointing to chart, and (4) looking up at child.

Miss Straton's basic personal repertoire is: (1) clasping hands together, and (2) unclasping hands. Her secondary personal repertoire is: (1) placing elbow on table, (2) placing tip of finger under chin, and (3) crossing arms.

Miss Straton has relatively few specific bodily motions that recur, and those motions in her repertoire involve only a limited portion of her body. Her personal repertoire is particularly small, for among all the case study teachers she uses the lowest number of personal motions. Of these motions we can say that they are almost imperceptible, such as the simple clasping of her hands. Similarly, her recurring specific instructional motions most often involve a minor movement of the head rather than a flourish of the arm; she is a nodder rather than a pointer. She appears, in fact, rather aware of how she uses her body; her motions almost seem studied and often seem intentional.

Beverly Straton's verbal repertoire is also restricted. Her basic verbal repertoire is: (1) says "Now" to introduce an action, and (2) reacts with "O.K." Her secondary verbal repertoire is: (1) directs the children "So write it again," and (2) reacts with "That's right."

The most distinctive feature of her speech is the sentence patterns she uses. She generally projects well-constructed questions, sometimes containing a statement the students are supposed to complete.

There are no "ah's" or "uh's" in her performance; again, as some other teachers, she pauses before important words and especially between major thoughts. Her tone of voice is that of composure and calmness, which also is reflected in her moderate speaking pace. We can thus say that the studied quality of her physical actions is paralleled with a studied verbal performance.

Looking at her overall activity, we note (1) an about average amount of total motion, (2) a slightly below average amount of physical motion, and (3) an about average amount of verbal activity. When we look at her instructional-personal ratio, however, we find that her ratio is 90.4 : 9.6. The ratio of the entire case study group is 77.9 : 22.1. Within this dimension, Miss Straton's ratio represents the extreme case.

Miss Straton's conducting-acting-wielding ratio is similarly distinctive, a ratio of 60.9 : 3.8 : 35.3, compared to an average ratio of 62.5 : 8.8 : 28.7. She is the lowest among the teachers in acting motions and makes above average use of wieldings. Focusing on her conducting motions, we see the lowest use of motions to obtain attending behavior; focusing on her acting motions, we see no pantomiming and almost no illustrating. When we turn to wielding, we note there that her per cent of direct and instrumental wieldings is highest among the teachers, whereas her per cent of indirect wieldings is low.

Miss Straton's structuring-soliciting-responding-reacting ratio is markedly different; she is highest in reacting moves, lowest in structuring moves. She makes almost no structuring or responding moves, falling into the soliciting-reacting-soliciting-reacting routine. She is about average in use of non-verbal motions to carry on these functions; but interestingly enough when she does structure or respond, she never does so non-verbally.

Miss Straton has a lesser tendency to employ Patterns B and D. Basically her teaching can be characterized by Patterns A and E. Finally, looking at how her own performance varies from one occasion to the next, we find greatest inconsistency in (1) the number of her instructional motions, and (2) the number of wielding motions. She is extremely consistent from lesson to lesson in making few personal motions.

For the teacher or teacher-in-training, we raise these questions:
1. Is nodding as effective as pointing? Why or why not?
2. Hypothesize as to why Miss Straton's use of wielding is higher than the other teachers'.
3. Miss Straton tends away from non-verbal illustrating. Give some examples of physical motions that can be used to illustrate.
4. Miss Straton has limited non-verbal and verbal repertoires. What are the advantages and disadvantages of this aspect of her style?

### Mr. David Rosen: Grade 4

Mr. Rosen's basic non-verbal instructional repertoire is: (1) looking around or surveying the class before calling on a student, (2) pointing to a child to indicate who is to recite, (3) pointing to a child to begin, (4) moving index fingers up and down to emphasize, and (5) making hand motions to illustrate. His secondary non-verbal instructional repertoire is: (1) pointing with chalk, (2) drawing on board to illustrate, (3) writing on board, (4) nodding at child to recite, and (5) climbing onto a stool, where he perches.

Mr. Rosen's basic personal repertoire includes: (1) placing hand in pocket, (2) taking hand out of pocket, (3) shifting his weight from one foot to the other, (4) bouncing up and down in place on toes, and (5) stepping from one side to the other. His secondary personal repertoire is: (1) jiggling coins in pocket, and (2) adjusting his position on the stool.

Mr. Rosen's repertoires are most interesting to consider. First, he has the tendency to illustrate and emphasize with his own characteristic hand gestures and to use the board to illustrate pictorially. Second, he likes to perch on a stool while teaching. Third, his personal motions center around his feet and his pockets, but are not excessive. (His instructional-personal ratio is close to average.)

Characteristic features of his basic verbal functioning include: (1) reacting with "All right" and repeating student's answer, and (2) beginning with "Now." His secondary verbal repertoire includes: (1) reacting with "Right," and (2) calling students "Folks."

Mr. Rosen has unique linguistic patterns. His sentences often do not have verbs or subjects as in: "Three black . . . does anybody in the class three black shirts or something to let these people wear?" He commonly employs contractions, particularly "gon'na" and "wan'ta" and flavors his speech with "uh's" and lengthy pauses. His emotions show in his voice.

When we look at his number of motions of each type, we discover that Mr. Rosen has a high activity level and a non-verbal orientation. He is above average in total activity and in amount of physical motion but below average in verbal activity. He makes many more non-verbal motions to serve a pedagogical function than any of the other case study teachers, and he employs more of Patterns D and E (totally non-verbal)—an overall non-verbal tendency.

Rosen's conducting-acting-wielding ratio is unique among the teachers—55.2 : 17.6 : 27.2, as compared to a mean ratio of 62.5 : 8.8 : 28.7. The man is more an actor than any of the other teachers; more than the others he uses his hands to illustrate and emphasize. But he does not role play.

One of the unique facets of Rosen's style is his greater tendency to structure and to respond; although he follows the general pattern of high proportion of solicitations and reactions, he structures and responds more than the other case study teachers. Oddly enough for a teacher who generally appears to be non-verbally oriented, his motions that serve to structure and respond are always verbal. It is primarily in his solicitations that his non-verbal proclivity shows up.

A fifth distinctive characteristic of Rosen's style is his variation in the number of motions used. From one teaching period to the next, he varies substantially in the number of (1) non-verbal motions, (2) verbal motions, (3) instructional motions, (4) personal motions, (5) conductings, (6) actings, (7) wieldings, and (8) patterns.

For the teacher or teacher-in-training, we raise these questions:

1. What possible relationships exist among Mr. Rosen's non-verbal orientation, his speech characteristics, and his tendency to illustrate with his hands?
2. Under what conditions would non-verbal illustrating be most important as a teaching strategy?
3. Rosen likes to perch on a stool to teach. What advantages does this posture have?
4. Rosen uses more responding moves than other case study teachers. Does this indicate anything significant about his classroom atmosphere?
5. Within the school Rosen was thought of as a "creative teacher." What is there about his style that may have contributed to his reputation?

### Mr. William Lambreck: Grade 5

Mr. Lambreck's basic non-verbal instructional motions are: (1) tapping bell before lesson, (2) walking to the board, (3) writing response on board, (4) underlining response on board, (5) picking up book, (6) looking down at book, (7) looking over or surveying class before selecting someone to respond, and (8) gesturing with hand toward child who should respond. His secondary non-verbal instructional repertoire includes: (1) stretching neck toward child who is reciting.

Mr. Lambreck's basic personal repertoire includes: (1) shifting book from one hand to another, (2) rubbing the cover of the book, (3) smoothing down pages of book, (4) leaning on desk, (5) placing leg on other knee, (6) straightening out crossed leg, (7) clasping hands, and (8) placing hand under chin. His secondary personal repertoire includes: (1) twirling ring on finger, (2) placing finger in mouth, and (3) rubbing lips.

We are not exaggerating if we say that Mr. Lambreck's non-verbal motions are almost totally limited to those we have listed in his repertoires, for typically he walks across the front of the room, book in hand, looking at the book to find the next question to ask, surveying the class, gesturing to a student to respond. At times he leans against the desk, left foot propped on his right knee. At other times he walks toward the board to record an answer.

Lambreck's basic verbal repertoire is: (1) to react, "Right" or "All right"; (2) to solicit for recitation, calls the child's name; and (3) to get attention, "May I have the attention of the whole class?" His secondary verbal repertoire includes: (1) to react, "Correct"; (2) to solicit, "Do you think that . . ." or "What do you think . . ."; and (3) to give sequence, "Now." Characteristics of his speech that are most readily observable are:

1. *Speed:* he speaks very rapidly when he directs a question, slows his pace when giving an explanation, and interjects pauses for emphasis.
2. *Tone:* he speaks decisively and with a sense of authority.
3. *Syntax:* he speaks in standard English patterns, using short direct sentences, e.g., "Take out your reading books. Now let's think for a moment. The topic is space. Why do you think I have chosen this topic?"

Mr. Lambreck is the most active of all the case study teachers. He makes more verbal motions during ten minutes of teaching—158 compared to a mean of 118. Likewise he makes more physical motions—671 as compared to a mean of 525. His personal motions are also more numerous; this is indicated by his instructional-personal ratio of 72.3 : 27.7, as compared to an average of 77.9 : 22.1.

Focusing on William Lambreck's conducting-acting-wielding ratio, we find a ratio of 59.6 : 4.5 : 35.9 as compared to a mean ratio of 62.5 : 8.8 : 28.7. It is obvious that a distinctive feature of his style is his higher than average use of wielding motions. When we look at the way he wields, we also find something unique; he tends to use an atypically high per cent of indirect wieldings. This fact is supported by one specific aspect of his non-verbal repertoire: Mr. Lambreck tends to hold a book and look at it as a guide in his teaching. Each time he looks at a book, his number of indirect wieldings goes up. We also find distinctive aspects about the way Lambreck uses conducting and acting. He uses very few conducting motions that attempt to obtain attending behavior and very few acting motions that emphasize. He does not make role playing motions.

William Lambreck's structuring-soliciting-responding-reacting ratio is 9.7 : 70.5 : 2.6 : 17.4, as compared to a mean ratio of 7.6 : 65.5 : 2.6 : 24.3, the major unique feature being a lower per cent of reacting moves and a slightly higher per cent of soliciting moves. It is within the verbal/non-verbal dimension that this feature becomes most pronounced. Lambreck rarely reacts non-verbally; rather he uses non-verbal devices to solicit.

The way Bill Lambreck uses move patterns is also distinctly his own. First, he alone was observed using an abortive pattern. Second, he prefers verbal patterns, Patterns A and B, over non-verbal patterns, Patterns D and E. This preference is supported by the fact that he, of all the teachers, uses the smallest number of non-verbal motions to serve a pedagogical function. A verbal orientation perhaps?

Mr. Lambreck is generally not an internally consistent teacher. His own performance varies extensively from one occasion to the next in number of motions, especially in number of personal and instructional motions, in number of verbal motions, and in number of conducting motions. This is interesting when we remember that he does not vary in the specific motions he uses—the motions in his repertoire.

For the teacher or teacher-in-training, we raise these questions:

1. What factors may cause a teacher to vary in the number of personal and instructional motions he uses from one occasion to another?
2. Should a teacher react every time a child gives a response?

3. Both Mr. Lambreck and Miss Straton use few conducting motions to obtain attending behavior. Are there any other features of their style that may account for this?
4. What are the advantages (disadvantages) of having a high activity level?
5. What are the advantages (disadvantages) of repeating exclusively the same specific motions in one's repertoire?
6. What are the advantages (disadvantages) of a teaching style that incorporates a high level of indirect wieldings (reading) by the teacher?

**PART II**

*Improving the Way
Teachers Move*

Chapter 5

# *Experimenting with Non-verbal Strategies*

Rotate the channel selector knob on your television set. On one channel the latest hit-recording star is doing his "thing." That "thing" may superficially be labelled "singing," but it is obvious that the performance involves far more than the production of a sequence of harmonious tones and related words. The recording star sings with his whole body—his torso gyrates rhythmically, his hands gesture to emphasize and to illustrate, his head is thrown skyward to express emotion.

Turn to the next station. There Red Skelton is doing his "thing"—a pantomime in which he wordlessly projects the trials and tribulations of a woman squirming into a tight girdle. He wiggles his flexible frame, stretching and then contracting his body. He pulls and tugs as each square inch of Red Skelton gets into the act.

Move to a third channel. Watch an actor forcefully plunge his right hand into a bulging pocket, move his head furtively from side to side, and slink down a dark alley, while another actor pulls his body close against the wall, every muscle taut, not moving an inch.

These performers—the singer, the pantomimist, the dramatic actor—understand that meanings can be communicated without words. Each motion is studied and deliberate. The head slowly drops forward to express sorrow; the hand is extended to point to some desired goal; the body is perched casually on a stool to communicate relaxation. Few extraneous motions take place, for the performer is aware not only of what he is saying but also of what he is doing.

Compare such purposeful motion to the motions of the teachers we have described. In the space of a twenty-minute lesson, our teacher fiddles with his tie, scratches his head, pushes back his chair, adjusts his glasses, places his hand in his pocket, paces back and forth, and so on. In addition, he points to a student, surveys his class, writes a child's response on the board, pulls down a map, nods his head. Yet regardless of whether his motions are of a personal nature or are related to the instructional process, the teacher is generally unaware of how he is using his body or whether his motions are reinforcing the meanings he is attempting to communicate; he is probably not using his physical motions purposefully as an integral part of his instructional strategies.

Today, however, we live in a technological age in which, with the spin of a dial, the child has spread before him skilled performances by Red Skelton, Carol Channing, Engelbert Humperdinck, the latest "in" rock group, or even Mae West on the Late Show. These performers, who have mastered the art of motion, pose stiff competition to the teacher. In meeting the competition, the teacher perhaps needs to borrow some of the actor's tricks of the trade; he needs to study how to use physical motion to reinforce or even to substitute for verbal communication.

## STRATEGIES OF THE ACTOR

The actor perceives his body as an instrument for expressing creative ideas. According to the Stanislavski method of acting, there is a strong connection between the psychological and physical in a human being; in every physical action there is always something psychological.[1]

Chekhov suggests that in the welding of mind and body, the actor blends four components into his actions: ease, form, beauty, and entirety.[2] He proposes that the actor must "use lightness and ease as a means of expression."[3] Similarly, Selden states that "the actor's gestures should be clean cut, free, natural, and spontaneous."[4]

Form is a second aspect of motion mastered by the actor. Quintilian, a Roman instructor of eloquence, teaches that "mastery of the art of gesture will not allow the hand to be raised above the eyes or to fall lower than the breast."[5] Selden directs that "gestures with a bit of a curve to them are commonly more effective than straight ones."[6] To

---

[1] Sonia Moore, *The Stanislavski System* (New York: The Viking Press, 1965).
[2] Michael Chekhov, *To the Actor* (New York: Harper & Row, 1953), pp. 13–18.
[3] *Ibid.*, p. 13.
[4] Samuel Selden, *First Steps in Acting* (New York: Appleton-Century-Crofts, 1947), p. 65.
[5] Marcus Fabius Quintilian, "Action and Delivery," *Actors on Acting*, Toby Cole and Helen Krich Chinoy, editors (New York: Crown Publishers, 1957), p. 29.
[6] Selden, *First Steps in Acting*, p. 65.

Selden, the hands share with the mind the ability to communicate purely intellectual ideas—they signal, they write, they point, they mark out this and that; they shape and control things in the environment.[7] In Quintilian terms, the hands almost speak.[8]

Beauty of motion must also be mastered by the actor. The actor's job is to translate an idea or theme into motions that convey meaning and that, at the same time, uplift and inspire the audience. The theme may be ugly or unpleasant, but the actor must aesthetically communicate that theme by applying "beautiful means." From Chekhov's point of view, the actor must have control over the form of his motions: floating, flying, radiating kinds of movement; yet, equally important, he must execute these motions sincerely, simply, harmoniously, with strength, with color, and with gentleness.[9]

In the final production, the actor must blend all of his separate moves to produce a total, unified effect. Chekhov suggests that the actor does this by stressing the essentials, by keeping in mind the main sequence of events. This aspect is what Chekhov calls "entirety," and it is this quality that holds the audience's attention.[10]

## STRATEGIES OF THE TEACHER

It goes without saying that the average teacher does not know how to use his body with the ease, form, beauty, and entirety considered so essential in communicating meanings by those who are experts in communication—the professional performers. This premise gives rise to the question: How can the teacher use his body more effectively as an instrument for expressing ideas? In this section we shall attempt to answer the question by considering non-verbal teacher behavior in terms of strategies developed in the theater.

### *The Set and the Props*

The set on which the teacher works is a matter of tradition; basic props include a teacher's desk and chair, students' desks and chairs, chalk boards and bulletin boards, bookcases and cabinets for storage, and in the elementary grades perhaps a piano. Although the teacher can form his basic props into any design that he desires, his physical activity is limited by the traditional desk-chair conception of the classroom. The props allow him to stand and to walk, to sit on the chair,

---

[7] *Ibid.*, p. 53.
[8] Quintilian, "Action and Delivery," p. 29.
[9] Chekhov, *To the Actor,* pp. 13–18.
[10] *Ibid.*, p. 17.

to lean on the desk, to sit on the desk. We suggest that schools need an up-dating of props to increase the options available to teachers.

What can these props include? Mr. Rosen adds to his "set" a high stool on which to perch. This device, borrowed from the repertoire of Perry Como, gives the performer an air of relaxation. When the stool is introduced into the classroom, it helps the teacher acquire that relaxed state so typical of Perry Como performances. At the same time the higher level of the stool allows him to maintain eye contact with students, even those seated in the back of the room.

In her second grade Mrs. Higgins uses a scatter rug and a hassock to give herself greater flexibility in moving. She sits on her hassock to tell or read stories to the children, who sit or lie on the "listening rug."

Another primary school teacher we know brought into her classroom a colonial-style, high-back rocking chair. She believes that by conducting discussions and by storytelling from her rocking chair, she maintains an informal, yet quiet environment.

At a higher grade level, we can obtain the same effect by borrowing a prop that is such an integral part of television "talk shows." Such interviewer-discussers as Merv Griffin and David Frost make use of a pedestal, swivel-type, contour arm chair. This chair makes it possible for a person to swing first in one direction, then in another. It enables an individual to prop his arms in a relaxed position. Why not have three or four chairs like this in a classroom for discussion situations?

### *The Expressive Hands*

The hands can serve the teacher in many of the same ways that they serve the actor. First, the actor uses his hands to describe, particularly size, shape, relative position, and state of motion. An expressive motion of the hands can say, "It is large," "It is round," "It is up here," or "It crawls along." These are ideas the teacher as well as the actor must communicate.

Gesture also has a use to support statements of logical relationships: a comparison, a contrast, a hypothesis. With a movement of the left hand the performer or the teacher can indicate "In this instance . . ."; with a movement of the right hand the performer indicates "In that instance . . . ." Likewise a gesture of the left hand can support "If this . . .", and a similar gesture of the right hand can support "Then that . . . ." The synchronized use of the two hands helps in making the distinction between the two parts of the comparison, the contrast, or the if-then relationship.

To make a point more emphatically the hands come into play. Forcefully, the actor or teacher gestures to suggest that this is what he is stressing—which words are most important.

The gesture also has its use to indicate the person or object to which reference is being made. In the theater such movement serves two purposes: to add emotional tone and to add clarity. The actor brings his hand in toward himself as he says "I do not believe it" and extends his hand outward toward his friend as he continues "You would not do that." The actor points toward a child as he says, "I gave it to her" and his gesture indicates whom he means. The teacher can make use of similar gestures carried out in as purposeful a way as the actor.

The actor uses personal motions as intentionally as he uses gestures that illustrate, focus, emphasize, or direct. F. Cowles Strickland in *The Technique of Acting* gives an example from the portrayal of Hamlet; in playing Hamlet the actor purposefully fingers the crucifix hanging around his neck to communicate to the audience that he is a man with strong religious beliefs.[11] The teacher too can turn his personal motions, perhaps those that are an integral part of his being, into effective teaching strategies. He can slowly and deliberately push up his glasses as he looks at a child who is not attending; by doing this he communicates "I see you very clearly." Or he can jiggle the coins in his pocket to communicate "I am waiting for you." Or the female teacher can even finger her pendant necklace in a gesture that means "H'm . . . that's an interesting point!"

In gesturing, the hand can be held in a variety of positions—the palm turned upward with fingers extended, the palm upward with fingers slightly curled, the palm downward, the palm perpendicular or at an angle to the floor, the palm turned to the audience, the back of the hand turned to the audience. Each of these theatrical positions of the hand has a place in the classroom. When the teacher wants to call a halt to the interaction, the palm turned toward the class is appropriate. When the teacher wants the noise level lowered, he can employ the downward position of the hand. When the teacher illustrates a sequence of steps to be carried out—"First, we will . . . . Next, we will . . . . Finally, we will . . . ," the back of the hand, turned to the class and moved a step closer to the speaker as each part of the sequence is introduced, is appropriate. The palm upward with fingers slightly curled can be used to say "Come here," whereas a similar gesture but with fingers extended can be used with "Give it to me."

In theatre arts, students learn specific techniques for hand gesturing. They learn that any gesture is composed of three parts: the approach, the stroke itself, and the return. Let us first consider the approach, the movement that carries the hand from its home base, the typical position of the hand at rest, to the point at which the actual gesturing takes

[11] F. Cowles Strickland, *The Technique of Acting* (New York: McGraw-Hill, 1956), p. 178.

place. The location of that home base determines how large the approach must be. Such a performer as Jack Benny, who uses his hands extensively in gesturing, often holds his arms bent at a ninety-degree angle and allows his thumbs and index fingers to touch slightly; as a result, he can approach a gesture smoothly and easily from this central position. He can move his forearms without leading awkwardly with his elbows; he can move his wrist first and keep his elbow close to his body as good gesturing technique demands. He does not need to move rapidly, for he has relatively little distance to cover before making the stroke itself.

Compare the Jack Benny approach to the approach of the teacher who characteristically stands with arms folded in front of his body or the teacher who clasps his hands tightly behind his back. The hands of these teachers are not available for free, uninhibited motion; and as a result their approach to the gesture is liable to be awkward, time consuming, and jerky.

The actual stroke is what communicates meaning—it is what describes, emphasizes, indicates object or person. It precedes slightly the word or words it accompanies and involves a slight suddenness of action. The arm then returns to the base position, completing the gesturing cycle. About the stroke of both teacher and actor we can ask: Does it really communicate meaning?

Some actors precede their major gesture with another action that gains attention. They put down a book or pick up an instrument before making their meaningful gesture.[12] This is a dramatic technique that the teacher can adapt. In doing a demonstration experiment, the teacher can dramatically pick up a match and hold it still for an instant before striking it. That instant of stillness focuses attention. Or the teacher can pick up a book, slip his finger into a marked place, and then dramatically open to the spot from which he wants to read. Or he can use such larger motions as closing the door, pulling down a map, climbing onto his high stool, moving his chair to a different location to become the focus of student interest.

### Vocal Pointing

Pointing is the actor's device to bring special emphasis to a thought, line, or word. One way of pointing is to highlight specific words with greater vocal stress. For instance, let us consider the sentence: "I didn't eat the cake." There are several ways of pointing this sentence. I can say, "*I* didn't eat the cake," and suggest that it must have been someone

[12] Jerry Blunt, *The Composite Art of Acting* (New York: Macmillan, 1966), p. 306.

else. Or I can say, "I didn't *eat* the cake," and imply that although I didn't eat it, I did do something to it. I can also say, "I didn't eat the *cake*," and in this case imply that I may not have eaten the cake but I did eat something else.

Not only does the actor point a word or line vocally by changes in stress but he also points by changes in rate, in volume, in pitch.[13] He speaks rapidly; he speaks slowly. He shouts; he whispers. His voice is high; his voice is low. To juxtapose two extremes provides a contrast that effectively draws attention to the thought or builds up to a climax.

The teacher can also point lines and words through changing the rate, volume, or pitch of his voice. The teacher who wants one line to stand out may speak that line more slowly than he has spoken the preceding lines. Or he may speak that line less loudly than he has spoken the preceding lines. Or he may even deepen his voice to point that particular line. This device indicates to the student that these lines are especially significant.

### The Dramatic Pause

The dramatic pause is a particular pointing device that the comedian has refined to a high degree of perfection. The pause to him generally means complete inaction; both verbal and non-verbal activity come to a halt. Watch two performers, Benny and Gleason, work together. Benny, known in his stage character for his "cheapness," has just offered to throw a party to celebrate Gleason's loss of weight and asks Gleason how to arrange the party. Gleason responds: "Our parties are very *informal*. First, you rent a hotel . . . ." Then comes the dramatic pause. Both men become physically still. The humor of suggesting that Jack Benny hire a hotel sinks in!

The teacher can employ the dramatic pause as purposefully as does the comedian. He can use it simply when he says "Look here . . . ." As he speaks, he can point to the place on the map, hold his hand in a deliberate way, and wait. His pause in word and body motion allows the students time to focus on that map.

The pause can be used after a question has been asked and before the student respondent is indicated. It can be used after a significant remark has been made. And as with the comedian, it can be interjected just after the punch line.

---

[13] Strickland, *The Technique of Acting*, p. 177.

## INCORPORATING THE STRATEGIES INTO TEACHING

We have described specific acting strategies that have a place in the classroom. We now raise a related question: How can the teacher incorporate these strategies into his own teaching?

### *Pre-planning Non-verbal Strategies*

When a teacher plans a lesson, he may consider: (1) what he hopes his students will learn, (2) what general procedures he will use, (3) what materials he will need, (4) what activities he will carry out, (5) what his opening remarks will be, (6) what his key questions will be, and (7) how he will evaluate student growth. Rarely, however, does he plan how he will use his body.

It is, of course, as unwise to pre-plan each bodily motion to be carried out in a lesson as it is to plan each remark to be made. First, there is need for spontaneity in one's teaching. After all, we in education do not work from a prepared script in the way that an actor does. We take on-the-spot direction and clues from our students; we watch for non-verbal clues emitted by students, and our own non-verbal clues often are a reaction to student behavior. An experienced teacher, for instance, can interpret the meaning of almost imperceptible motions his students make—a slight turning of the body, a small change in facial expression, a movement of the fingers, a change in posture—and will alter the verbal and non-verbal clues he is generating.

Second, it is physically impossible to plan all of one's non-verbal clues; there are far too many motions a teacher makes in just ten minutes of teaching even to consider the idea.

Yet, there are certain aspects of our non-verbal performance that logically have a place in our lesson planning. The teacher can, for example, plan how to use his hands to introduce a major concept; consider whether he will attempt to keep his body motionless at a key point in the lesson; think about whether to perch on a stool, stand, or sit at his desk during a discussion to establish a specific classroom mood; or consider whether he will point at a map with his finger, with a piece of chalk, or with a pointer. These motions are major ones related to important props, overall position, and pivotal points in the lesson. In this respect they can be pre-planned.

### *Practicing Non-verbal Strategies*

The teacher who uses his hands only minimally to facilitate the communication process, who does not employ vocal devices to point lines, or who does not use the pause to heighten effect can begin to improve his own non-verbal teaching by doing as the actor does—by trying out lines and motions. Similarly, the teacher who has not incorporated role playing motions into his teaching can try out pantomiming activities in hypothetical situations. Then when situations arise in his classroom in which pantomiming, vocal pointing, gesturing, pausing are appropriate, he will feel more at ease, and bodily motion will seem natural to him.

For practice purposes we include two series of exercises. The first series is a group of statements, some typical of instructional statements of teachers, others taken from children's stories. The reader should try projecting the statements and try accompanying the words with gestures. Each statement should be read several times with different effects attempted at each reading. The second series is a listing of pantomime situations. The reader can see if he can role play the situations.

*Exercise Series I.* Practice saying:
1. The first step is to describe how we move. The second is to analyze our description.
2. Everyone should sit down immediately.
3. The most significant point is that the war lasted over eight years.
4. The larger it gets, the more awkward it is to handle.
5. I'm concerned about your lack of attention.
6. The first diagram on the board indicates the relationship between weight and volume.
7. At the top of the classification scheme we have man; at the bottom are the one-celled organisms.
8. "They went looking high and low
   And every place a dog might go."
   (Ludwig Bemelmans, *Madeline's Rescue*, Viking Press, 1953.)
9. "And when he came to the place where the wild things are, they roared their terrible roars and gnashed their terrible teeth and rolled their terrible eyes and showed their terrible claws."
   (Maurice Sendak, *Where the Wild Things Are*, Harper and Row, 1963.)
10. "Pretty soon there was a subway going back and forth underneath the Little House."
    (Virginia Lee Burton, *The Little House*, Houghton Mifflin, 1942, p. 26).
11. "Ping was always careful, very, very careful not to be last, because the last duck to cross over the bridge always got a spank on the back."
    (Marjorie Flack, *The Story about Ping*, Viking Press, 1933, p. 5).

12. "They took their coasters to the top of a hill. 'Get-ready—get set—go!' they called."
(Lorraine and Jerrold Beim, *Two Is a Team,* Harcourt, Brace & World, 1945.)
13. "Up hill and dale, in great leaps and bounds.
The carpet raced on like a hare chased by hounds."
(Rex Parkin, *The Red Carpet,* Macmillan, 1948.)
14. "So (the monkey) said to himself, 'Just as soon as the tiger is about to pounce on the camel—I will drop this cocoanut on his head.' And all the while the beautiful camel walked gracefully down the road, turning her pretty head this way and that, while the sky got brighter and brighter."
(Jack Tworkov, *The Camel Who Took a Walk,* Dutton, 1951.)
15. "Once upon a time a little lighthouse was built on a sharp point of the shore by the Hudson River. It was round and fat and red and jolly. And it was Very, Very, Proud."
(Hildegarde Swift and Lynd Ward, *The Little Red Lighthouse,* Harcourt, Brace & World, 1942.)

*Exercise Series II.* Pretend to:
1. Push a heavy box across the room.
2. Slip on a banana peel.
3. Open a door with your arms full.
4. Put up a card table with a collapsing leg.
5. Sneak down a narrow alley.
6. Swim against a current.
7. Hang a picture.

Chapter 6

# Generating Non-verbal Clues

In his classroom performance a teacher is continually generating clues as to what he holds important, what standard of behavior he expects, what kinds of participation he wants, what quality of work he will accept. Some of a teacher's clues are verbal; others are non-verbal. Some clues are generated consciously by the teacher; other clues are not even within the teacher's sphere of awareness. But regardless of whether the clues are verbal or non-verbal, regardless of whether the clues are consciously or unconsciously being generated, the students are molding their behavior in reaction to those clues.

Although teacher clues mold student behavior, not all teachers are knowledgeable about the clues they are generating—especially about their non-verbal clues. This is possibly an outgrowth of the verbal society in which we live—a society that stresses verbal production and generally ignores the intricacies of non-verbal activity. Schools traditionally have been concerned with teaching written and spoken communication; only rarely have they attempted to teach ways of working the body to facilitate and to serve the communication process. Teachers, who themselves have been educated in a verbal school situation, often do not function with non-verbal consciousness, and thus are unaware of the relationship between their verbal and non-verbal communication patterns.

Our work with video tapes of actual classroom performances of teachers supports this contention. We have identified from the tapes certain fundamental problems associated with non-verbal clues generated by teachers and with the related use of verbal clues. The problems we have identified are of four types: (1) a problem of contradictory clues, (2) a problem of insufficient non-verbal clues, (3) a problem of excessive non-verbal clues, and (4) a problem of ineffectual clues. Let us examine each of these problems.

## CONTRADICTORY CLUES

One teacher's performance has been captured on tape as she asked: "What is the sound of 'q-u' in this word?" She was looking at her class as she asked the question, and reached up simultaneously to point at the word written on the board. But an interesting thing happened. Since she was not looking at the board, she pointed to a different word than she intended—the word "noisy" rather than the word "quiet." There was no response from the class. She restated her question; still no answer. Then one little girl responded: "You mean 'quiet' not 'noisy,' Mrs. . . ." "Of course, it's 'quiet,' Marcia. What is the sound of 'q-u'?" And then Marcia gave the answer the teacher wanted.

During this episode, the teacher never did realize that she was generating two different sets of clues—a verbal set and a non-verbal set that were contradicting one another. The verbal statements were communicating one question; the non-verbal conducting motions she was using to facilitate or support her words were actually developing a different focus. The end product was lack of clear direction and resulting confusion for the students. In this instance, the confusion was only momentary and really not serious, for direction was quickly restored. Yet in other instances a more serious situation can result from conflicting clues.

A more serious example of contradictory clues is taken from the performance of one teacher recorded on video tape. The following is an excerpt from an introductory creative writing sequence:

| The Teacher Says | The Pupils Say | The Teacher Moves |
|---|---|---|
| "I'd like you to think about—what it would be like if you were a snowman. What would you do—or what would you say? Think of some different things that you would do or say." | | Points to temple with index finger to illustrate concept of thinking. Taps temple slightly on "think." Walks toward class group. Brings down hand from temple with index finger extended to emphasize "you were a snowman." Uses index finger and arm in a circular motion to emphasize "what you would say." |

| The Teacher Says | The Pupils Say | The Teacher Moves |
|---|---|---|
| | | Makes another circular motion for emphasis on "think." Uses hand motions for emphasis on "do" and "say." Drops hand to hip. Turns to look at children. |
| "What are you going to do if you need a word spelled? What are you going to do?" | | Raises hand to illustrate. Surveys the group. |
| | Children call out: "Raise your hand." | |
| "You're going to raise your hand, and I am going to look around—and put it on a piece of paper." | | Pushes hand forward and higher to illustrate process of raising hand. On the words "piece of paper" holds up fingers in shape of piece of paper. |

After a short period of time had elapsed, a child who had begun to write called out, "Miss. . . ." And the teacher went to him. Her non-verbal response to the child's call was in distinct conflict with her previous verbal and non-verbal clues—to raise the hand.

We have encountered numerous examples of teachers' generating contradictory clues. We remember one teacher who, after projecting a rather difficult question, suggested: "Let's all think about that for a moment." Then she went to the board, erased it, and wrote a new list of topics. Surely her physical actions at this point did not reinforce her words; rather they communicated something entirely different. The students *knew* that she really was not asking them to think. She just needed time to prepare for the next questioning sequence. A studied pause, coupled perhaps with our case study teacher's gesture of pointing to her head, would have been more in tune with the content of her words.

Another teacher tended to end his comments with the question "Do you understand that?" His words encouraged student participation and projected what might well be called an open environment. Yet no students responded with a question. Why? It was evident to the observer that the teacher's non-verbal activity and even facial expressions belied his words. As he remarked "Do you understand that?" he made an emphatic pointing gesture at the students that communicated clearly to them "You had better understand that or else!" The stern expression on his face combined with this recurring gesture resulted in an environment that was far from open. Non-verbally it was closed.

In still other situations we have seen teachers whose words communicate, "this is the important element" or "this is an urgent matter." Yet they simultaneously use no gestures to emphasize, and their overall bodily stance communicates anything but a sense of importance or urgency. In this instance, contradictory clues coming from their verbal and non-verbal behavior legitimately raise a question in the students' minds. Is this really so important or so urgent?

In sum then, contradictory clues involve the sending of two conflicting messages—a verbal message that says one thing and a non-verbal message that implies the opposite. The result can be confusion for the students or, as we say today, a turning off of both messages.

## INSUFFICIENT NON-VERBAL CLUES

Approach a friend, and, pretending you really don't know, ask: "What is a spiral staircase?" We can almost guarantee that your friend will resort to circular hand motions to get his point across. In this instance, to paraphrase a well-known expression, a gesture is worth a thousand words.

Each teacher should pause and ask himself whether he (1) is generating too few non-verbal clues to carry on pedagogical functions, (2) is generating too few non-verbal clues to support his verbal communication, or (3) is excessively inactive physically in the classroom. If he answers "Yes" to any of these questions, he should think about how he can substitute that gesture for those thousand words.

For instance, one teacher whom we observed had six statements, written on the board. He pointed to the first, read it, and asked, "What is incorrect about this statement?" "Marie?" He then pointed to the second statement, read it, repeated his question, and called on a second youngster. He repeated this sequence for each of the four successive statements. Actually, the teacher did not have to repeat himself after the second statement. He could simply have pointed to a statement, surveyed the class, and then gestured to a student to recite.

By substituting non-verbal for verbal activity, the teacher gains certain instructional bonuses. First, when he turns off his audio performance and turns on his video style, he is changing his previous routine completely; this change adds interest and variety. Second, children hear their teacher's voice all day long; it is a wonder they do not "turn him off" more often than they do. When the teacher solicits non-verbally, the ever-present voice disappears from the scene. Third,

# Generating Non-verbal Clues 77

the action is speeded up; the time that was lost in repeating the question is salvaged. This speeding up is significant in instruction, for needless repetition may be one factor that brings boredom.

Other instances when bodily movement may functionally have a place in instruction to speed up the action and add variety in the teaching patterns are when (1) the teacher smiles as a reaction to a student response, rather than saying, "Very good"; (2) the teacher wrinkles his forehead in doubt in reaction to an incorrect student response; (3) the teacher points at the child who will come to the board, rather than calling him by name; (4) the teacher picks up his book and holds it so all the children can see it, rather than saying, "Let's all take out our spelling books"; (5) the teacher claps his hands to get attention, instead of speaking; and (6) the teacher walks toward a child who is misbehaving, rather than saying, "Freddie!"

The second question a teacher needs to ask himself is whether at times he is failing to support his verbal clues with non-verbal motion. For example: (1) Could he point his index finger at the cabinet to which he refers and say, "It's there"? (2) Could he hold up his hands to illustrate the size of the paper he means as he says: "The small paper"?

Failure to support words with non-verbal clues can produce both wordiness and lack of clarity as is indicated in these two examples. The teacher who points to the cabinet probably could get by with only the statement "It's there." Without the gesture he may have to string word after needless word and ramble, "It's there . . . The drawer in the back cabinet . . . No, no, not that one . . . the one farther over . . . No, not that one either . . . over one more . . . Keep going. That's it." The teacher who holds up his hands in the approximate size of the paper similarly is making more clear which size he wants his class to select.

A third question that a teacher should raise about his own classroom behavior relates to his overall production of non-verbal clues. Is the environment that he produces so bereft of non-verbal stimuli that emphasis and stimulation are lacking and attention lags? The teacher who moves his head or arm to emphasize is telling his students: "This is the important factor." He is giving his students an additional clue not supplied by the overly-verbal teacher, and at the same time he is stimulating student activity. Similarly non-verbal activity forces a student to look at the speaker if he wishes to get the message. With the student's eyes focused on the teacher, greater eye contact and possibly heightened attention are maintained.

In short, we suggest that minimal non-verbal stimuli generated by the teacher may have a number of results—wordiness, lack of clarity, lack of variety, lack of stimulation, and lack of emphasis.

## EXCESSIVE NON-VERBAL CLUES

Anything carried to an extreme can become distracting—and so too with non-verbal clues generated in classrooms. Three kinds of bodily motion have a possible negative effect: (1) inappropriate motion, (2) distracting personal motion, and (3) over-stimulating motion.

### *Inappropriate Motion*

There is a time in any classroom when a spreading stillness produces an overall effect that reinforces what the teacher has been doing. This stillness is one of both physical and verbal quiet. The teacher pauses, holds his body motionless, and waits. We have observed teachers do this to discipline pupils. Seeing a group of children in a state of semi-disorder, the teacher stops in mid-sentence and focuses on the children in a manner that suggests "We suspend all activity in this class until you emotionally rejoin us."

There are some teachers, however, who find a complete suspension of activity rather disturbing to themselves. They rush in to fill the void with a non-verbal motion or a word and lose the effect they are attempting to achieve. Often they suggest that, after all, they cannot wait forever, and they have paused what seems to be an interminably long time.

A junior high school teacher has told the writers that, when he begins a year, he uses the technique of spreading silence to communicate to his students that he requires their attention on the work. With one class he did become concerned about the amount of time being "wasted" by waiting, so with his wrist stop-watch, he clocked the time. During the first few sessions, the total time spent waiting came to four out of sixty minutes; after the first week, it was only thirty seconds.

The complete absence of motion can also be used to heighten interest and to emphasize. After one teacher whom we observed poses a complex problem, he typically cuts off his verbal motion and leans motionless against the desk. His stance implies that he too is contemplating the intricacies of the problem and seems to be encouraging his students to follow suit. Another teacher we observed makes rather lengthy pauses in his activity after something significant has been said. Again his lack of motion suggests that what has been said is worthy of extended consideration. Still another experienced teacher seems to call a halt to his own motion after activity in the class has reached a rather high point and has stayed at this high level for a long period of time. His halt seems to imply: "Let's stop a minute and catch our breath."

**Distracting Personal Motion**

Excessive personal motions may indirectly affect a teacher's success. We talk now of the teacher who may perpetually scratch, fiddle, rub to the point that students become highly aware of this manifestation of personality. Yet the teacher himself is almost totally unaware of his activity.

Our contention that specific, excessively recurring personal motions can be distracting to students is reinforced by an anecdote recounted by an experienced teacher with whom we discussed physical motion. He recalled a college professor who continually reached his right arm behind his head and scratched his left ear; students in the class were held spellbound by the professor's gymnastic-type motion. Many years later it was this activity that was the single fact remembered about the professor's teaching.

**Over-stimulating Motion**

We have observed teachers who are extremely active both verbally and non-verbally. Their bodies are in perpetual motion; they walk up and down the aisles; they sit down; they stand up; they pace back and forth; they point; they nod; they move their hands in circles, in triangles, and in indeterminable patterns. From their mouths comes a steady stream of discourse.

One result of a highly active teacher performance is a high tension level. The teacher's almost continual state of motion prevents the students from relaxing. Such teachers find it hard to leave youngsters alone during writing sessions; throughout such a "quiet time" the bombardment of motion continues, and the observer wonders how children concentrate in this environment.

There is no emphasis in a highly active teacher performance. The teacher who pumps his hand or index finger and nods his head on every other word has used all his ammunition in the skirmishes and has nothing effective left for the major battle except more of the same. Under these conditions, the youngster has no guide as to what is significant other than the content of his teacher's statements, i.e., when the teacher actually says "There are three important factors" or "This is the fundamental reason."

## INEFFECTUAL CLUES

What do we mean by an ineffectual clue? A teacher nods his head at a child to indicate that the child is the one to recite. But no eye contact with the child occurs simultaneously, so three children in that immediate area call out the answer. Another teacher, in an attempt to tell a child where to find a pair of scissors, makes a vague gesture to the front of the room. This diffuse non-verbal motion proves as unhelpful as the first teacher's nod. Motions that do not communicate what the teacher intends—motions that just don't work—we term ineffectual.

Very often a motion or series of motions used extensively will become ineffectual. A supervisor of new teachers with whom we spoke told us about a beginning teacher who repeatedly said "Sh-h-h-h" and shook his head to reinforce his words. Since he generated this motion over and over again without following through in any perceptible way, his motion had become ineffectual.

It is in the context of ineffectual motion that we can look at the teacher's overall stance, his posture, his walk, his manner of sitting. Few teachers probably have viewed themselves in action and raised such questions as: (1) Is my bodily stance communicating what I want it to communicate—concern, interest, enthusiasm? (2) Is my manner of sitting communicating what I want to communicate—relaxation, informal friendliness, enjoyment? (3) Is my manner of walking communicating what I want it to communicate—determination, excitement, diminishing tempo?

Chapter 7

# *Factors Related to the Production of Non-verbal Clues*

As we have observed teachers in classrooms and have analyzed their behavior on tapes, extreme differences have become evident among teachers in the use of non-verbal motions. From our study we have identified a series of factors that we hypothesize are related to the differential production of non-verbal clues by teachers: (1) teacher personality, (2) student characteristics, (3) nature of subject being taught, and (4) instructional framework.

## TEACHER PERSONALITY AND NON-VERBAL CLUES

As a person am I highly active, normally active, rather passive? The way the teacher answers this question relates to his total activity level in the classroom. Teachers who in everyday living are highly active will probably carry that activity into the classroom and generate numerous clues, both verbal and non-verbal. In contrast, the less active person carries his state of being into the classroom and generates fewer clues.

Whether these clues tend to be verbal or non-verbal again depends on whether the teacher has a verbal or non-verbal orientation in everyday living. Sometimes, too, the person who has problems functioning verbally resorts to more non-verbal devices. We noted that the teacher with a poor vocabulary and limited facility with a variety of sentence patterns may rely more heavily on non-verbal communication than the teacher who can put words together with little effort.

The teacher's self-concept also influences his production of nonverbal clues. What kind of self concept must a teacher have in order to pretend that he is an elephant or a bunny? Some people would feel foolish with arms extended, pumping their heads up and down like an elephant. Others would feel that such an action would be beneath them, would be inappropriate for someone with their authority, status, or poise. Their concept of self would not permit them to participate in this type of rather childish activity.

We are not implying that such activity *is* childish. We remember a college professor of biology, a Harvard Ph.D., who would become so involved in the animals or insects he was describing that he would hunch over, place his index fingers to his head as antennae, pretending to be a grasshopper, or he would roll his arms in undulating motions simulating ocean-living organisms caught in the tides. He was considered an outstandingly interesting professor.

Another professor who was recently voted by the students as the best teacher on his campus has an extensive repertoire of role playing motions. An English professor, he runs around the classroom in order to describe a run-on sentence; in essence he becomes the run-on sentence. To make more vivid a dangling participle, he "dangles" himself over the side of a desk. Speaking of himself and his teaching, he claims that he is absolutely uninhibited in his teaching; if a motion adds to the instruction, he will use it.

Generally speaking, adults tend to be more inhibited than children and don't use role playing in their everyday activity to the extent that young children do. Perhaps this inhibition accounts for the small number of teacher role playing–pantomiming gestures encountered in classroom observations. The adult teacher may be afraid to express himself physically in a creative "let's pretend" way.

Of course, too, the personal gestures a teacher brings into the classroom often are those he tends to employ in out-of-class situations. If he pushes up his glasses "in teaching," he probably does it "in living" as well. If he puts his hands into his pockets and jiggles his change, he is probably a jiggler at heart. And so also with mannerisms—the personal mannerisms manifested in teaching often are visible outside the classroom.

## THE STUDENTS

A second factor that influences the kinds and number of physical motions employed by a teacher is the nature of his student population. We suggest that three characteristics of the student population are of primary importance: (1) age and grade level, (2) verbal level, and (3) emotional level.

### Grade—Age Level

According to Heinz Werner, the young child organizes his world in terms of activity; in a global situation or a field he perceives "things of action," rather than the characteristics of objects or the specific elements. His conceptions of time and space are concrete and egocentric. Time to him is breakfast, midday nap, or even snow (winter), and he uses his own body in determining possible relationships in space.[1] Piaget calls this period of intellectual development the "preoperational stage"—a stage in which the child by manipulating the world establishes "relationships between experience and action." Piaget suggests this stage generally ends around the fifth or sixth year, when the child learns to manipulate symbols and is able to represent his external world symbolically, even though he must still rely heavily on the concrete. It is not until age twelve that the child moves into a stage Piaget terms formal operational—a stage characterized by the ability to handle abstract relationships without dependency on the concrete.[2]

For the young child who organizes his experiences around "things of action," overt physical motion by the teacher is a fundamental aspect of instruction. The child delights in "let's pretend," and the teacher who is a leader in the activity needs to pretend along with him. Try reciting for a group of young children the Mother Goose rhyme "Humpty Dumpty" while sitting on the edge of a desk and pretending you are Humpty Dumpty. When you get to "Humpty Dumpty had a great fall," pretend to collapse. The children will be with you every syllable of the way, and soon they will be reciting and pretending they too are Humpty Dumpty.

For the high school student who can become more involved in abstract ideas, such overt physical action is not always so essential to learning. These students can find enjoyment in taking an idea and looking at it from many different angles or within many different contexts. They analyze and synthesize. They evaluate and interpret. In such functioning, non-verbal motion "takes a back seat."

---

[1] Heinz Werner, *Comparative Psychology of Mental Development* (New York: John Wiley & Sons, 1948), pp. 1–506.
[2] Jean Piaget, *The Psychology of Intelligence* (London: Routledge & Kegan Paul Ltd., 1964), pp. 123–155.

### Verbal Level

Walter Loban has described the language of the disadvantaged as not utilizing the "full potential" of our language. By this he means that linguistically disadvantaged children make only limited use of the sentence patterns available in the English language and the patterns they do use are relatively simple or even incomplete. In addition, they base their speech in the present tense, rarely employing the future or the past, and their speech relies heavily on concrete references.[3]

We propose that, although the teacher must continually converse with linguistically disadvantaged youngsters to help develop language facility, non-verbal devices have a higher priority than with linguistically able children. A gesture of the hands to illustrate and make more concrete, a movement of the hand to draw a rough sketch on the board, a pointing to each syllable written on the board may serve to improve communication between a teacher and student whose language patterns are limited and who relies heavily on the concrete.

### Emotional Level

In discussing the education of brain-damaged children, Robert Travers, an educational psychologist, writes:

> One way of handling such children, so that conditions become more favorable to learning, is to attempt to lower the level of arousal by lowering the amount of stimulation provided by the environment. This is the opposite of what is done in the case of the normal child, who is generally placed in a highly stimulating environment in order to raise the arousal level.[4]

Do non-verbal teacher motions add stimulation to the classroom environment? There is little question in our minds that certain kinds of teacher motions do stimulate students—motions used to illustrate, to pantomime, to emphasize, to focus attention.

But do we always want to liven up a lesson? Not according to Travers; much stimulation for the brain damaged child has a negative effect. That this is also true of students with emotional problems is a logical deduction to make. Our observations support the deduction. Emotionally disturbed youngsters can get carried away when the

---

[3] Walter Loban, "A Sustained Program of Language Learning," in Iris M. Tiedt and Sidney W. Tiedt, eds., *Readings on Contemporary English in the Elementary School* (Englewood Cliffs: Prentice-Hall, 1967), pp. 22–30.

[4] Robert Travers, *Essentials of Learning: An Overview for Students of Education* (New York: The Macmillan Co., 1963), p. 182.

teacher uses stimulating non-verbal motions, especially those involved in role playing. After all, it is rather exciting to see the teacher pretend to be an elephant, and even the up-and-down motion of the teacher's hand used to emphasize can be disturbing. In this environment, a more studied use of physical motion seems requisite.

### THE SUBJECT

Our third hypothesis is that the teacher's conception of the subject being taught is a factor determining the kind and number of non-verbal clues he generates. This is slightly different from suggesting that the nature of the subject itself is the determining factor, for it is possible to conceive of a subject in many different ways. For instance, there are still numerous teachers who conceive of science as a body of facts to be acquired. To them, therefore, science teaching may basically involve reading and talking about these facts. Translated in terms of non-verbal activity, this means the production by the teacher of motions that wield indirectly—reading motions.

On the other hand, teachers who conceive of science as an experimental method of inquiry are more likely to teach science through experimentation. Their conception translated into non-verbal activity means more motions that wield directly—motions involving the actual manipulation of equipment and materials—and motions that serve to conduct participation in the interactive situation.

The study of mathematics can also be structured in different ways. The elementary school teacher who conceives of math as a way of finding answers to specific problems may see mathematics teaching as explaining how to do the problems. This teacher uses chalk board conducting motions as he does the problems at the board, and from their seats the children follow along with each step. Another elementary school teacher who see mathematics as a means of understanding numerical relationships is more likely to rely on the manipulation of real objects and employ more direct wieldings as well as conducting motions used to control participation.

The elementary English teacher who believes we should describe language as it is currently spoken is going to differ too from the teacher who believes that Latin grammar adequately describes the English language. The first teacher is more likely to work with sentences the children produce orally to develop notions of how words are put together in English. The second teacher is more likely to draw upon sentences from the language arts book that will exemplify generalizations based on traditional grammar. And again there will be resultant differences in the way they apply conducting, acting, and wielding motions.

Similar distinctions can be made about the teaching of an introductory foreign language. The teacher who believes that language is how we speak it will tend toward an audio-lingual approach, in which he develops conversations based on real objects or pictures brought into the classroom. Another teacher, who believes that written communication is more basic than oral communication, will begin with the written word. The first approach relies to a lesser extent than the second on use of books and again there will be a resulting difference in non-verbal teacher motion—especially in the use of wielding motions.

## THE INSTRUCTIONAL FRAMEWORK

What aspects of the classroom instructional framework can affect the teacher's use of non-verbal motion? Based on data developed about our case study teachers, we hypothesize that influencing factors include: (1) the physical arrangement of the classroom, (2) the technological devices and materials available to the teacher, and (3) the teacher's conception of a positive classroom environment.

### The Physical Arrangement

There are many ways physically to organize a classroom. Some teachers use a cluster scheme, pushing desks into clusters of four or five. Other teachers apply a horseshoe design. Still others retain the scheme based on parallel rows. In each of these designs, the teacher's desk can be placed in any number of positions—in the back of the room or in the front, in the middle of the room or to one side. But it is obvious that each combination mandates certain kinds and numbers of teacher motions. For instance: (1) A teacher's desk located in the back of the room may mean more walking motion for a teacher when he wants to get materials during a chalk board–oriented lesson. (2) A desk set in the middle of a horseshoe scheme may mean more turning first in one direction and then in another to maintain eye contact with the total group. (3) A row scheme may mean that a teacher needs to walk to the front of each row when he distributes supplies. (4) A cluster design, in which each cluster includes children grouped together for some instructional purpose, means that when it is time for small group instruction the teacher needs only to carry his chair to that location before beginning group work.

### Technology and Materials in Use

We suggest that a second facet of the instructional process that affects the teacher's use of non-verbal motions is the technological devices and materials being employed. Imagine the classroom in which the primary teaching tools are: (1) books, (2) paper, pens, pencils, and (3) chalk boards and chalk. Next imagine the classroom with the additional tools: (4) maps, globes, (5) simple scientific equipment, and (6) flannel and magnetic boards, pocket charts. Then imagine the classroom in which not only these tools are employed but also: (7) tape recorders and record players, (8) overhead and opaque projectors, (9) filmstrip and motion picture projectors, and (10) closed circuit T.V. cameras.

Each tool we add to a classroom makes instruction slightly different. The teacher has to generate different verbal and non-verbal clues—particularly non-verbal clues—, since there are new devices to be manipulated and each device almost forces a teacher to perform certain physical motions.

Among the case study teachers, we found that the teachers who are most inconsistent in the number of motions performed from one lesson to the next are the ones who periodically use technological devices in their teaching. When we compare a lesson involving use of a device with a typical "talk" lesson done by the same teacher, we discover greater variance in the use of physical motion than when we compare a teacher's "talk" lesson with another of his "talk" lessons. The use of the device dictated a different motion sequence.

One example from the behavior of our case study teachers stands out in our minds as an instance in which a piece of equipment influences non-verbal activity. Mr. Rosen uses a tape recorder rather often in his teaching to record student opinion. Under these conditions, he non-verbally conducts by pointing the microphone in the direction of the child he wishes to recite. This gesture, not noted in any of his lessons not involving a recorder, makes it unnecessary for him to have his own voice taped.

Other examples of motions dictated or made possible by use of special equipment are: (1) the teacher uses the flicking on of the tape recorder to mean "Attention"; (2) the teacher turns out the lights to focus attention on projected material; (3) the teacher focuses attention by pointing at a transparency that rests on the overhead projector; (4) the teacher picks up the globe and hands it to a child to support the question "Where is India located?"; and (5) the teacher assembles a ring stand, asbestos mat, flask, propane torch in preparation for a science demonstration. In each of these situations, the introduction of different teaching tools requires the teacher to produce different physical motions.

### Teacher Conception of a Positive Classroom Environment

One teacher we observed never personally distributes supplies nor collects papers; she never touches a projector or a machine. Students have responsibility for these tasks, for she believes that the classroom is a place to develop responsibility and initiative.

One of our case study teachers, Mrs. Higgins, sometimes directs a child: "Stan, you be the teacher and ask the next question." Then she goes over to a desk and sits motionless while Stanley assumes the role of teacher. This teacher believes that children should raise as well as answer questions.

Mr. Rosen, another of the case study teachers, does not demand student attention during a discussion lesson. If children don't want to participate, they can get up and do whatever they want. He makes no motions to draw them back into the group, for he feels that what his students have on their minds may be as important as what he is discussing. Noise level is not his concern.

Mr. Lambreck believes every minute of instruction should be planned. He knows exactly what questions he will ask, and all students are expected to listen and participate, for each question is part of a sequential development of an idea.

Each teacher has his own unique, idealized conception as to what makes up a positive classroom environment, and it is in terms of this ideal that he teaches and then judges his own teaching behavior. In his idealized conception of instruction are notions about the part the children should play in instruction, the amount of individual attention that should be given, the kind of disciplinary climate he wants to achieve, and the nature of the pupil-teacher relationship he wants to maintain. There are conceptions of a lower order relating to how much ventilation there should be, whether children should be allowed to choose their own partners, or whether pencils can be used instead of pens.

How do such idealized concepts of instruction affect the non-verbal clues teachers generate? Referring to the four teachers just described, we find that the first teacher uses few direct wielding motions; the second has low total activity during periods of student leadership; the third rarely if ever makes conducting motions that attempt to obtain attending behavior, whereas the fourth teacher uses many indirect wieldings, as he often refers to his plan book.

## QUESTIONS FOR THE TEACHER

The non-verbal clues a teacher generates are dependent upon numerous factors—some related to the teacher himself, some related to the students, some related to the subject being taught, and still others related to the materials being used. The teacher who seeks to improve his own non-verbal classroom performance can begin by considering how these factors relate to his own behavior. He can look at his own teaching and ask:

1. Do my non-verbal motions complement my verbal clues?
2. Do I use what seems to be an excessive amount of non-verbal activity? a sufficient amount?
3. How effectual are the physical motions I use?
4. Are the personal motions I make distracting?
5. Am I self-conscious in the use of role-playing motions?
6. Do I tend to have a verbal or a non-verbal orientation?
7. Am I gearing my use of non-verbal activity to the age level of my students? their emotional level? their verbal level?
8. What do my non-verbal clues indicate about my conception of this subject?
9. Does the physical arrangement of my classroom mandate an excessive use of motion?
10. What do my non-verbal clues indicate about my conception of the instructional process?

Chapter 8

# *Selecting from Among Non-verbal Options*

When we analyzed the typescripts of teacher, non-verbal, classroom behavior, we were impressed by the wide variety of non-verbal clues being generated by teachers. There is not just one way to conduct or to act or to wield. Rather there are numerous options open to a teacher at any single point in a lesson. For this reason we believe that good teaching involves a wise selection from among options. We say "wise selection," because the teacher should make his determination based upon understanding of his own personality, of the student group with which he is working, of the instructional process, and of the nature of the subject being taught.

Because there are so many determining factors that influence a teacher's production of non-verbal clues, there is no one mode of behavior we can hold up as a model to emulate. Each teacher develops a unique non-verbal style. This style is developed to a high level of sophistication when the teacher purposefully selects from among options a motion pattern he deems most productive and carries through that motion with some degree of finesse.

In this chapter we consider some of the options open to the teacher who has developed enough awareness of and control over his non-verbal functioning to use motion consciously and purposefully in the classroom.

We refer the reader to Appendix B, where he will find an inventory that will help the teacher to study his own non-verbal behavior in terms of the options described in this chapter.

## CONDUCTING OPTIONS

Conducting refers to motions that control participation and obtain attending behavior. We propose that there are numerous conducting options available to the teacher to carry out these tasks.

### *Controlling Participation—Indicating Participants*

One facet of controlling participation is indicating which student or students are to participate at a given moment in the lesson. Possible non-verbal motions that can be selected to indicate specifically who the participant or participants will be include:

1. smiling at the child who is to participate
2. focusing one's eyes on the participant
3. orienting the body in the direction of the participant
4. nodding at the chosen participant
5. pointing at the participant with
    a. finger
    b. whole hand
    c. stick
    d. chalk
    e. microphone
    f. book
6. walking toward the participant
7. handing the pointer, chalk, book, microphone to the next participant
8. touching the participant.

Verbal motions that can perform the same task and are, therefore, viable options include:

1. saying "Yes?"
2. saying "Please?"
3. calling participant's name
4. making such statements as:
    a. "Do you have an answer?"
    b. "What do you think?"
    c. "Do you want to react to that?"[1]

These options can be seen as alternate means of performing; they can also be seen as simultaneous means. For instance, a teacher may walk toward, point his hand at, call the name of the participant he has chosen, making use of several options at the same time. Actually teachers tend to make several conducting motions "in unison," as was seen by the relative use of move patterns among the case study teachers. Move Patterns A (verbal/non-verbal) and D (non-verbal/non-verbal) were most frequently used.

The options through which teachers can indicate participants differ in three major respects: in definitiveness, in size, and in speed. First, some modes indicate very precisely who is being chosen. Calling a child's name, touching a specific child, pointing directly at a child are options less open to confusion than smiling, nodding, or orienting the body in the direction of the participant. When the teacher wants to make absolutely clear whom he is indicating, it would seem wise to select from among the more definitive options rather than from among the less specific ones; this would be particularly true during periods of disciplinary stress. In addition, when the teacher employs less definitive options, it often pays for him to accompany the motion with an action that adds specificity—such an action as making eye contact with the student he has selected.

Of course, there are times when the teacher does not want to specify who is to participate. Rather, he wants all the students to respond in chorus. The teacher can generate non-verbal, verbal, or both verbal and non-verbal clues to communicate this "modus operandi" to the pupils. He can extend both arms, palms upward, fingers slightly curled. Or he can extend one arm and sweep it slowly in front of himself. Or he can select a verbal option and say "Everyone," "All together," or "Anyone." These clues indicate that total class participation is desired.

Secondly, motions indicating participants differ in size. Walking toward a student is a larger gesture than pointing. Pointing is a larger gesture than smiling. Smiling is a larger gesture than making eye contact. There are times in classroom interaction when a teacher wants minimal physical activity to maintain a mood of quiet or stillness as part of an overall effect he is attempting to achieve. For instance, if a very serious discussion were in progress in a high school class, such a still, contemplative mood would be appropriate. And under such a condition a small gesture would be necessary. On the other hand, if a teacher is trying to build up excitement and to inject liveliness into the lesson, the opposite would be true; a larger gesture would be in order.

Thirdly, motions indicating participants differ in the rapidity with which they can be carried out. A simple nod accompanying the calling of the student's name obviously takes less time to perform than walking toward the child. When a teacher wants to maintain a fast pace, it would be wise to select an option that does not take a considerable amount of time. Conversely, if he wants to slow the pace to achieve a special effect, such as heightened emphasis, a more time-consuming option would be in order.

Often specific motions indicating the next participant are preceded by a motion that seems to be an integral aspect of non-verbal teaching behavior. This motion is the one we have called "surveying the class," moving the head to make eye contact with several students in the group. This gesture is preliminary to motions that indicate who should be the next participant. It is generally accompanied by a pause in verbal activity. Sometimes too this preliminary conducting activity is accompanied by more overt action such as walking toward the class from a position by the chalk board. The motion "surveying the class" serves three fundamental purposes in instruction by communicating three messages to the students: "Everyone think about the question," "Who wants to participate?" and "I am making up my mind who shall participate."

### Controlling Participation—Reacting to a Participation

As he conducts the class, how can a teacher react to a student's participation? There are a number of non-verbal possibilities. He may:

1. use facial expressions: smiling, frowning, grimacing, grinning, wrinkling his brow, raising his eyebrows
2. shake his head: slowly, vigorously
3. shrug his shoulders
4. clap his hands
5. make the O.K. sign with his fingers, forming an "O" by touching thumb to forefinger
6. put his hands to his face
7. hold his head
8. scratch his head
9. pat child on back
10. move his hand from respondent to another student who has hand up to recite.

Verbally, he may react with such words as:

1. *Positive:* Good, fine, O.K., correct, excellent, very good, great, terrific, wonderful, you're on the right track;
2. *Negative:* Not quite, no, that's wrong, I don't think so;
3. *Intermediate:* Just about, almost, you're half right, we're getting there.

He may react even more specifically, his reaction suggesting precisely how the student has been right or wrong. For example, the teacher may react as one college professor of ecology recently did: "In your analysis you identified the major point—man is a part of his environment, not separate from it." Then too in a verbal reaction a teacher may just repeat the student's answer, implying by repetition that the answer is correct.

The options available for teacher reacting differ in time, in specificity, and in emotional tone. Let us first consider the time factor. Maintaining a certain expression and nodding can occur concurrently with a student response. As the student responds, the teacher can keep his head nodding in agreement or shaking in disagreement; likewise, he can smile encouragingly. In instances when students need encouragement as they participate, such non-verbal reactions have a fundamental role to play. When the teacher wants the student to keep speaking to delve more deeply, concurrent non-verbal reaction seems to be effective. A waving motion in which the teacher's fingers move in a direction from the speaker to the teacher can communicate the message.

By contrast, a verbal reaction can occur only after the child has made a response unless, of course, the teacher interrupts. Yet a verbal clue has the advantage of allowing a very specific reaction that can guide the child in his thinking. We can indicate precisely in what way the child was right or wrong. We can suggest to him—"Focus more on the author's style," or "Your point is relevant, but is that the most significant factor?" or "But have we considered all the major elements of plot development?" or "Do you think *all* fish have that characteristic?"

A third difference among reacting options is the emotional tone that can be communicated. A facial expression has potential to communicate warmth and understanding, whereas a nod of the head can communicate much less feeling. Words too can be delivered so that assurance, concern, or even irritation is part of the message.

That the emotional tone of a teacher's reaction is fundamental to continued participation of many students is indicated by comments of college students. When we asked a group of college students whether they were at all hesitant about speaking out in a class, more than half expressed some concern about opening their ideas to public criticism. They expressed fear of being told they were wrong or more specifically of appearing foolish before their peers. Such comments suggest how important facial expressions are in reacting-conducting situations. The teacher may have to say "We're not quite getting at the point. Let's try again" when an answer is wrong, but a brief, simultaneous smile can further say "I appreciate your attempt."

**Controlling Participation—
Reacting to Student Non-verbal Clues**

Just as the teacher is generating non-verbal clues so is the student. Students facially express opinion and feeling; they nod and shake their heads; they gesture with their hands; they orient their bodies; they focus their eyes, they stare into space, and they glance at one another; they get up and walk; they move their chairs and desks; they fiddle with objects and with themselves.

The experienced teacher who knows his students generally can "read the message" sent by their non-verbal activity. One teacher knows, for instance, that an almost imperceptible cocking of her head means that Vickie has the answer and wants to recite, whereas a changing of position in her chair is Susan's sign of readiness to participate. He knows that a certain kind of expression on key students' faces means that the students generally are lost and are not getting the point, whereas another kind of expression is assurance that the point is generally understood. Likewise, he knows that glances at the clock, far away looks in students' eyes, continual shifting of positions in seats are signs of student unrest and lack of interest; that continual student eye contact with the teacher and attentive posture probably mean greater interest.

The experienced teacher not only reads student non-verbal communication but also reacts to it. He may change the pace of the lesson; or on the spot he may reorganize what he is doing. He may look at his own watch and say "Yes, we have only ten minutes left to the period." He may point to Vickie or Susan as participant rather than the single child who has a hand raised.

**Controlling Participation—Responding to Students**

A student asks verbally or non-verbally if he may leave the room; the teacher responds by nodding his head and pointing to the door. Another student points at an open venetian blind through which the sun is streaming onto her face. The teacher responds non-verbally by nodding and waving his hand. When students ask questions that require only "Yes" or "No" answers, the smile or frown and the nodding or shaking of the head are possible modes of responding.

The kind of question projected by a student determines in large measure whether yes-no non-verbal conducting motions are applicable as a method of response. When the question raised is of minor significance in the overall success of the learning situation, non-verbal options are most appropriate. Why destroy the logical thought sequences in progress to say, "Yes, close the blind"? Why spoil an emotional tone that has been established to say "Yes, Jack, you may go to the boys' room"? The non-verbal option can serve the function without intruding on the real mission of the lesson as the verbal option would do.

Our two examples also indicate how important it is to establish non-verbal patterns through which youngsters can ask such routine questions as "May I open the window?" or "May I close the blinds?" or "May I go to the girls' room?" One teacher has students raise their hands made into fists to ask the last question; many teachers do not even require the question to be asked. The student simply signs his name on the board and erases it upon returning.

Another kind of question that can be answered non-verbally is one asking, "Where?" Where are the paper, the chalk, the stapler? The teacher, who knows the location of his supplies, can often answer simply by pointing or even by nodding. But for questions requiring a fuller answer the teacher has no non-verbal options that can perform the responding function. He must project a statement.

### *Controlling Participation—Focusing Student Attention*

Still another aspect of controlling participation is focusing student attention on what is significant at that point in the lesson. Non-verbal options that can help students focus include:

1. writing the significant point on the board
2. underlining a word or words written on the board
3. pointing to each word written on the board
4. writing over each word written on the board, perhaps using colored chalk
5. pointing to a chart, bulletin board display, or picture
6. pointing to a location on map or globe
7. putting words or letters into a pocket chart
8. pointing to person or object being discussed
9. pointing to a picture or statement projected by an audio-visual device
10. "tacking" word cards to chalk board with magnets
11. holding up the actual object (e.g., a rock, an insect, the globe, a microscope) being discussed
12. holding up a word card
13. holding up a picture
14. adding the key ingredient in a science demonstration.

Verbally teachers can focus attention with such remarks as "Here it is," "Look here," or even by repeating their own words.

Dramatic techniques are particularly effective as a means of focusing attention. One junior high school science teacher whom we observed would organize his discussion on finding volume so that a student sooner or later would say, "What we need is a large wooden cube we can cut into smaller square cubes to see the relationship between volume and external dimensions." The teacher would pause as if in thought, dash into his storeroom, reappear, dramatically hold up a large cube, and then nonchalantly remark: "I just happen to have one of those." This technique of dramatically producing the key object at the key moment can be used in numerous situations as a focusing device: (1) The teacher can have his key pictures turned over on his desk and produce them at the psychologically "right" moment. (2) The teacher can have a map pulled down over key material—diagram or statement—on the board; he dramatically "unveils" it. (3) The teacher can have a bulletin board that he is going to use as motivation for a lesson covered up with brown paper until the strategic point in the lesson. (4) The teacher can have the key interest object—an amusing puppet, a fossil of a shell, a map of under-ocean features, a graph—hidden away, to be dramatically exposed at the key moment. (5) The teacher can build a science episode on what will happen if we combine chemical x with chemical y or if we heat chemical z. The actual doing of the experiment, the combining or heating, becomes the climax toward which the lesson builds and can be carried off with dramatic effectiveness. The teacher reaches for the container of chemical x, slowly pulls out the stopper, reads the label, makes a pouring motion, then pauses in mid-air, asks "Have we considered everything?" When he finally pours, all eyes are on him.

### *Obtaining Attending Behavior—Total Class*

Verbally the teacher can say "Let us begin" or "Let us take out our history books" to obtain the attention of the total class, or he can just start to talk. Non-verbally, the teacher has many more options; he may:

1. close the door
2. flick the lights
3. tap a desk bell
4. pull down a chart or map
5. pick up his text book or lesson plan book
6. walk to the front-center of the room
7. survey the class making eye-contact

8. stand at attention
9. hold up his hand
10. tap fingers or pencil on desk
11. play a note on the piano
12. arrange his chair or stool and sit down.

The effectiveness of each of the options is dependent on the state of activity already present in the class and the amount of conditioning the students have had in responding to that option. If there is a high level of group noise in the class, words like "Let's begin" probably will be lost. Likewise, if children are preoccupied with assigned group activity, the teacher's standing in front-center of the class will probably not draw attention. However, tapping of a bell, playing a note on the piano, or flicking the light switch will communicate above the noise and despite student preoccupation with the task at hand.

When the teacher sets up certain basic routines that he tends to use over and over again, students become conditioned to attend when presented with specific non-verbal clues. One junior high school teacher we observed stands by the door as the children come in. When all have entered, he pulls the door closed with a rather firm bang, walks to his desk, picks up his attendance sheet, takes a position center-front. Even before he calls the name of any missing child, the students are quiet. They have been conditioned to expect that the teacher is ready to begin the lesson when he stands center-front. His quiet way of getting attention is effective here because the students are not preoccupied with another task and the existing noise level is minimal.

### *Obtaining Attending Behavior—The Misbehaving Child*

To gain the attention of a non-attentive child, the teacher has several verbal options open to him; he can:

1. call the name of the student
2. make statements to the student that range from simple reprimands to outright verbal chastisement. The teacher can simply ask, "Joyce, are you with us today?" or he can chastise, "Joyce, what is the matter with you? Pay attention, and stop fooling around!"
3. pause in the verbal activity.

Non-verbally he can:

1. orient his body toward and focus his eyes on the inattentive student
2. frown at the child

3. raise his eyebrows
4. wave his hand at the child
5. shake his head in the direction of the child
6. point his finger at misbehaving child
7. raise hand and arm in the direction of the child
8. snap his fingers at the child
9. walk toward the misbehaving child
10. put hand on desk of misbehaving child
11. sit down near the child
12. touch the child
13. touch the object the child is touching.

The options available for gaining the attention of a misbehaving child or a small group of non-attending children differ in the amount of distraction resulting for the other students in the class. One student teacher whom we observed recently must have realized this. As she conducted a reading group, she noticed that the child on her right was rotating a globe on a table between them, and was not reading the story. She simply put her hand on the globe and applied a pressure to stop the rotation. The boy removed his hand and focused on his reading. None of the other students seemed at all aware that the teacher had "disciplined" Freddie. Later the student teacher stood up and went to the other side of the reading circle to hold up some related pictures. After a short time, Freddie again began to play with the globe. The teacher promptly returned to her chair, tapping Freddie's shoe as she went by. Freddie immediately ceased his activity, but again none of the other children was aware of what had occurred.

There are two major advantages of using non-verbal motions to obtain attending behavior. First, non-verbal motion seems to make less of an issue out of minor inattention and does not put the child into the center of everyone's attention, a position the misbehaving child may very much desire. Rather the misbehavior is handled simply and quickly. Second, the non-verbal motion does not interfere with the on-going activity of the classroom. While the teacher is standing with his hand resting on the desk of the inattentive child or while the teacher is orienting his body toward and focusing on the child, the class discussion or activity can continue without disruption.

## ACTING OPTIONS

The second major non-verbal role of the teacher we have identified is acting. We have suggested that the teacher is acting when he uses his body to emphasize, to illustrate, and to role play. Again there is not just one way to emphasize, nor just one way to illustrate, nor just one way to role play. Rather there are numerous options from which the teacher can select according to the requirements of the moment.

### *Emphasizing*

To emphasize the teacher has available both non-verbal and verbal means. Non-verbally he can make movements of his hands, head, or feet; or he can use facial expressions to reinforce other motions. Specifically he can use his hands:

1. to make many kinds of gestures: up-and-down movements, jerky movements, waving movements
2. to pound on the desk
3. to point at self or person as when saying "I mean you."

Or he can use his head:

1. shaking it back and forth
2. nodding it up and down
3. moving it in indescribable patterns.

A third emphasizing option is use of feet; the teacher may:

1. walk
2. tap his foot.

Fourth, he may employ facial expressions to appear concerned, stern, happy, emphasizing the tone of his remarks.

Vocally for emphasis he can change the stress, speed, pitch, or volume of his speech; he can pause strategically. In addition, he can employ such specific words as important, basic, fundamental, remember, first. These words imply greater significance.

### *Illustrating*

To illustrate, the teacher has available three kinds of non-verbal options—hand gestures, foot motions, and head motions. Which of the options is applicable in a particular instance is dependent upon the nature of the concept or idea being developed. For instance, the hands can be effective in describing objects. They can be moved with a swaying, undulating rhythm to describe the movement of a bell buoy; or a sweeping, flattening motion of the hand can be useful in describing the continental shelf. Hand motions can also be effective in illustrating such processes as hammering, chopping, kneading, rolling, rubbing, scrubbing.

The feet come into play as illustrative agents for concepts, ideas, or processes involving the feet and rhythms. If the teacher is illustrating the beat of a march, tapping the foot is an option. If he is teaching how to move the feet when one is pitching a ball or when one is doing a particular dance step, actual foot motion is an applicable illustrative device.

Movement of the head is an illustrative option the teacher may select in place of hand or foot movement. For instance, a second teacher may well swing his head back and forth to describe the action of a buoy rather than employ the hand gesture. This type of activity would be especially useful when the hands are occupied with such other tasks as holding bulky pictures. Likewise, the head can be used instead of the feet to illustrate the rhythm of a particular kind of music; the head would be an especially good illustrative rhythm agent under conditions where visibility of feet is rather limited.

## Role Playing

When the teacher decides to role play or pantomime, he has chosen to involve the whole body in the action rather than selecting a simpler illustrative motion involving only the hands, feet, or head. As we have suggested already, a teacher can illustrate a buoy using only his head or only his hands to simulate motion. But it is possible to move the entire body rhythmically and to pretend that one is actually a buoy being tossed about in the water. Likewise, one could cup one's hand and "hop" to simulate the motion of a bunny. But it is also possible to hunch one's shoulders and actually hop across the room bunny style.

Role playing activity is more dramatic and probably more interest provoking than simpler forms of illustration. It is, therefore, most effectively used at key points in a lesson when we really want high student attention. Also, it is effectively used when we want students to become physically involved in the lesson. In the "bunny options" just cited— hand motion versus total body action—total body action is an appropriate choice when the teacher wants the children also to pretend that they are hopping bunnies.

In summary, we suggest that when the teacher decides to employ acting motions in the class, he has numerous options open to him. These possible ways of acting range from the use of a limited portion of the body as an emphasizing or illustrative agent to the use of the entire body in pantomiming.

## WIELDING OPTIONS

From our study of the wielding behavior of teachers, we project four major areas of decision making related to production of wielding motions in the classroom: (1) whether to employ direct or indirect wieldings in a particular instance, (2) whether to employ indirect wieldings involving reference to lesson plans and guides, (3) whether to involve students in wielding, and (4) when to wield.

### Direct Versus Indirect Wielding

In wielding the decision to be made is whether to wield directly or indirectly. Basically direct wielding involves the manipulation of concrete materials—tape recorders, globes, scientific equipment. Indirect wielding involves the act of reading or focusing on the printed word. The wielding options open to the teacher, therefore, are related to selection of materials. Each material has characteristics that make it a possible option in certain learning situations. For instance, books are a particularly good choice when we want students to form their own visual images and to exercise their imaginations, or when we want students to develop reading skills, or when we want students to get enjoyment from literature, or when we want students to read opinions and ideas of men of today and yesterday. Pictures are a particularly good choice when we want students to make logical inferences from a visual image, or when we want students to have an accurate visual image of an object or group of objects, or when we want to have a change of focus during a reading lesson. Phonograph records are a particularly good choice when we want students to listen to a musical composition performed by a professional group, or when we want students to hear a story told by an outstanding performer or to listen to another language spoken by a native, or when we want students to differentiate among audio stimuli, or when we want students to be stimulated creatively to write or express themselves, or when we want to establish a particular classroom mood. Pocket charts (charts with slots into which cards can be slipped) are a particularly good choice when we want to focus children's attention on words, or when we want to develop progressively each word in a sequence.

For each kind of material available—maps, projectors, tape recorders, television—a list of specific applications could also be proposed, because each of the media serves a special, rather unique function in instruction. Concrete materials have a place as do symbolic materials. Realia have a place as do representations. The teacher who wields wisely is not the one who selects the concrete in preference to the symbolic or the real instead of the representation; rather he is the one who purposefully selects the material that meets the needs of that particular learning situation.

### Indirect Wieldings and the Teacher's Plans

Another kind of wielding decision to be made by the teacher concerns the use of indirect wieldings in referring to lesson plans or to teachers' guides. Some teachers choose to read each of their questions from prepared plans and in so doing increase their indirect wieldings. Other teachers use the teachers' manual and sequentially ask questions from the guide.

One alternative is to study the material extensively before the lesson is given. Key questions to be asked may be noted in plan books, and questions in teachers' manuals may be studied ahead of time. But this material is only a framework in which the teacher operates during the actual lesson; then questions are projected spontaneously within the pre-established framework.

Another possibility is placing key questions on the board, projecting questions with the overhead projector, or distributing them on duplicated sheets. The teacher wields indirectly when he looks at the questions projected or written on board or sheet. Selection of this option introduces fewer indirect wieldings into the teaching than selection of the plan book–oriented alternative. It introduces more indirect wieldings than the spontaneous option.

Having children pose the questions is still another possibility. A teacher whose plans include this option will tend to use fewer indirect wieldings, as he is generally a listener and resource person.

Advantages of options that allow the teacher to focus most of his attention on his students rather than on his plans are greater eye-contact and more freedom to employ hand motions. The teacher who works from a plan book held in hand cannot react spontaneously, cannot gesture freely, cannot keep his eyes on his students. The beginning teacher who elects to rely heavily on indirect wieldings related to the plan book or teachers' guide may even lose control of his class, because children know when the teacher is focusing more on the book than on them.

### Student Involvement in Wielding

The teacher also makes decisions about who will do the wielding; he decides whether he himself will wield or whether students will take on the role of wielder. The teacher wields when he adjusts the window blinds, when he threads the projector, when he fills beakers, when he empties the pencil sharpener. Yet, we have observed some students performing these and similar acts; and, of course, when they do, the teacher's overall conducting-acting-wielding ratio is affected.

Then, too, students can carry out indirect wieldings normally reserved for the teacher. We observed a teacher who was running through a brief remedial exercise found in the book. Instead of picking up the book himself and calling the questions, he asked one student to serve as "questioner." The questioner read each of the questions in the exercise at a point indicated by the teacher's nod. Other students, of course, responded with the answers. But during the sequence the teacher never referred to his own book.

Several advantages accrue from involving students in instructionally related wieldings. First, involvement often produces a sense of belonging and of commitment to the undertaking. The student who sets up the overhead projector on which the lesson is based or distributes the books and paper becomes more a part of the lesson than if he sits at his desk while the teacher wields. Second, the teacher need not concentrate on the projector nor bend down to take paper from the cabinet. He can maintain greater eye control. Third, if the teacher has set up systematic routines for distributing supplies and for doing housekeeping chores, student participation in the routine is a learning experience in itself. This is especially true when the wielding is a technical one such as setting up a projector or lighting the bunsen burner. Fourth, students often enjoy involvement. Sometimes it is just the opportunity to get up and stretch that is enjoyed. Sometimes it is the ego-reinforcement of being able to wield that complicated piece of equipment that is enjoyed. And sometimes there is a positive feeling in being able to help.

Limitations on student involvement in wielding are age of the children, skill of students, and safety. First, students in early primary grades (K–2) are a bit young to help with technical tasks. Second, to assist with technical tasks, children need instruction to develop skill. Unless that instruction has been given previously, confusion can result —film all over the floor, projector focused at rear wall. The same can be said for establishment of routines for distribution and collection of supplies and materials. Unless systematic procedures have been previously developed, student wieldings can produce noisy confusion. Third, some wieldings involve an element of danger as, for example, closing the window with a long window stick when there are unprotected glass light fixtures in the room. The safety factor is a consideration in deciding whether to select an option involving student wielding.

## When to Wield

Wielding involves the manipulation of materials in the classroom and actions leading to manipulation of materials when that physical activity does not require student attention. For example, if the teacher threads a motion picture projector in order to show a film, students need not focus on his threading motions, which in this case are wieldings. If he is threading the projector to teach children how to manipulate the projector, however, then student attention on the task is requisite, and his motions are conductings.

Since students need not focus on the teacher's wielding motions, it is obvious that he does not have to wield at a specific time. He has a choice from among time options. In our example of the projector, if he has to do the threading himself, he can thread the machine even before the children arrive; he can thread it during a student work period, or he can thread it just before the film showing.

Likewise, if the teacher wants to write material on the board and student attention is not required, the teacher has a choice from among options: to write the material before the students come into the room, while the students are performing some other task, or just before using the material. Factors that influence his selection from among time options are: (1) other material that must be put on the board, (2) amount of surprise desired, (3) how full his own classroom schedule is, and (4) how good his disciplinary control is. If he has other material for a previous lesson filling the board, he must wait until that material has been used. If surprise is important, he must wait until just before the lesson or he must select another procedure allowing more surprise (e.g., projection of material with an overhead projector). If his own in-class schedule is filled with other instructional tasks to perform, he must do it ahead of time. And if he is having some disciplinary problems, he should not choose to write extensively on the board during the class period. His back turned to the class may pose too great a temptation for the misbehaving child to resist. When the teacher who cannot put the material on the board before class is faced with a disciplinary concern, he needs to question his own selection of material—the chalk board. Perhaps the duplicated sheet and the overhead projector are more suitable options from which to choose.

## Selection of Wielding Options

When the teacher wields, he chooses from among options; he chooses "what," "who," "when," and "how"—what material to wield, who will do the wielding, when to do the wielding, and how often he will refer to his plans. Yet these decisions are very much interrelated. Often a decision about what material to use limits the options relating to "who," "when," and "how"; and likewise a decision about "when to wield" may limit the options relating to "what" and "who." The teacher who wields with a high degree of sophistication is the one who has considered these interrelationships and selects options that meet the needs of the particular situation.

Chapter 9

# *Improving Teaching Via Descriptive Research: A Point of View*

We began our exploration into non-verbal dimensions of teaching by developing a category system by which to describe the way teachers move in the classroom. We then used the system to analyze the non-verbal performance of five case study teachers, which we recorded on video tape. This approach is based on a specific point of view that we hold—that adequate description of the teaching act must precede projections on improving teaching. This, in a sense, is a scientific approach to the study of teaching that follows the descriptive pattern established by such researchers as Smith and Meux (1962), Flanders (1965), and Bellack (1966). Researchers such as these have used either first-hand observation or recordings to supply data on the verbal activity of teachers. Working from these data, they have given us highly reliable descriptions of:

1. how teachers carry on such logical operations as (a) classifying, (b) defining, (c) explaining, (d) evaluating (Smith and Meux);
2. how teachers (a) structure, (b) solicit, (c) respond, (d) react (Bellack); and
3. how teachers (a) accept student feelings, (b) give praise, (c) accept, clarify, or make use of student ideas, (d) ask a question, (e) lecture, (f) give direction, (g) give criticism (Flanders).

The work of these researchers has centered on investigating verbal aspects of teaching, because the technique they have been forced to use—direct observation or tape recordings—has limited their study. Today, however, with the advent of video-taping techniques, a new and exciting era has dawned in the study of classroom activity; the educator can now rely on permanent records of both verbal and nonverbal patterns. The success of the technique, as a foundation for descriptive research, is seen in the work of Biddle and Adams (1967), who video-taped the performance of sixteen different teachers and described patterns of interaction in these teachers' classrooms.

We believe that describing teacher verbal and non-verbal performance as recorded on video tapes and analyzing that performance will ultimately be more productive in finding an answer to the question "How can we improve teaching" than will prescribing what teachers should do in classrooms. For this reason, even in our section on improving teaching, we have not prescribed one ideal mode of non-verbal teaching. Rather we have described numerous non-verbal strategies; we have suggested non-verbal clues that probably are non-productive; we have identified factors that seem to be related to non-verbal production; and, finally, we have projected conducting, acting, and wielding options open to the teacher. We have done this from the belief that the primary way to improve non-verbal teaching is for the teacher himself (1) to become more aware of his own non-verbal activity and the effect it has on his students; (2) to experiment with non-verbal strategies he previously has not attempted; and (3) to select purposefully from among options those conducting, acting, and wielding motions that meet the needs of a particular situation. This, then, is the role that descriptive research can play in improving the way The Teacher Moves.

# Bibliography

## PSYCHOLOGICAL FOUNDATIONS

Almy, Millie, Edward Chittenden, and Paula Miller. *Young Children's Thinking: Studies of Some Aspects of Piaget's Theory.* New York: Teachers College Press, 1966.

Burnshaw, Stanley. "The Body Makes the Minde." *The American Scholar,* XXXVIII (Winter 1968–69), 25–39.

Coats, W. D. and U. Smidchens. "Audience Recall as a Function of Speaker Dynamism." *Journal of Educational Psychology,* LVII (August 1966), 189–191.

Jersild, Arthur. *When Teachers Face Themselves.* New York: Teachers College Press, 1955.

Piaget, J. *The Psychology of Intelligence.* London: Routledge & Kegan Paul Ltd., 1964.

Polanyi, Michael. *The Tacit Dimension.* New York: Doubleday & Company, Inc., 1966.

Travers, Robert. *Essentials of Learning: An Overview for Students of Education.* New York: The Macmillan Co., 1963.

Vygotsky, L. S. *Thought and Language.* Massachusetts: The M.I.T. Press, 1962.

Wallack, Michael A. and Nathan Kogan. *Modes of Thinking in Young Children.* New York: Holt, Rinehart and Winston, Inc., 1965.

Werner, Heinz. *Comparative Psychology of Mental Development.* New York: John Wiley & Sons, 1948.

## COMMUNICATIONS

Brigance, William Norwood. *Speech Communication: A Brief Text Book.* New York: Appleton-Century-Crofts, Inc., 1947.

Ehrensberger, R. "An Experimental Study of the Relative Effectiveness of Certain Forms of Emphasis in Public Speaking." *Speech Monographs,* XII (March 1945), 94–111.

Hall, Edward T. *The Silent Language.* Greenwich, Conn.: Fawcett Publications, Inc., 1967.

Loban, Walter. "A Sustained Program of Language Learning." *Readings on Contemporary English in the Elementary School.* Edited by Iris and Sidney Tiedt. Englewood Cliffs: Prentice-Hall, 1967.

Ruesch, Jurgen and Weldon Kees. *Nonverbal Communication: Notes on the Visual Perception of Human Relations.* Berkeley and Los Angeles: University of California Press, 1961.

Shenker, Israel. "A New Study: Behavior While Talking." *The New York Times,* February 12, 1969.

## THEATRE ARTS

Blunt, Jerry. *The Composite Art of Acting.* New York: The Macmillan Company, 1966.

Boleslavsky, Richard. *Acting: The First Six Lessons.* New York: Theatre Arts Books, 1963.

Chekhov, Michael. *To the Actor.* New York: Harper & Row, 1953.

Kahan, Stanley. *Introduction to Acting.* New York: Harcourt, Brace & World, Inc., 1962.

Marowitz, Charles. *Stanislavski and the Method.* New York: The Citadel Press, 1964.

McGaw, Charles. *Acting Is Believing: A Basic Method.* New York: Holt, Rinehart and Winston, Inc., 1966.

Moore, Sonia. *The Stanislavski System.* New York: The Viking Press, 1965.

Oxenford, Lyn. *Design for Movement.* New York: Theatre Arts Books, 1952.

Quintilian, Marcus Fabius. "Action and Delivery." *Actors on Acting.* Edited by Toby Cole and Helen Krich Chinoy. New York: Crown Publishers, 1957.

Redgrave, Michael. *The Actor's Ways and Means.* New York: Theatre Arts Books, 1953.

Rockwood, Jerome. *The Craftsmen of Dionysus: An Approach to Acting*. Glenview, Illinois: Scott Foresman and Company, 1966.

Selden, Samuel. *First Steps in Acting*. New York: Appleton-Century-Crofts, Inc., 1947.

Strickland, F. Cowles. *The Technique of Acting*. New York: McGraw-Hill, 1956.

## THEORY AND RESEARCH ON TEACHING

Adams, Raymond S. and Bruce J. Biddle. *Realities of Teaching: Explorations with Video Tape*. New York: Holt, Rinehart and Winston, Inc., 1970.

Amidon, Edmund and Elizabeth Hunter. *Improving Teaching: The Analysis of Classroom Verbal Interaction*. New York: Holt, Rinehart and Winston, Inc., 1966.

Barr, A. A. *Characteristic Differences in the Teaching Performance of Good and Poor Teachers of Social Studies*. Bloomington, Illinois: Public School Publishing Co., 1929.

———. "The Measurement and Prediction of Teaching Efficiency: A Summary of Investigations." *Journal of Experimental Education*, XVI (June 1948), 203–283.

Bellack, Arno A., Herbert M. Kliebard, Ronald T. Hyman, and Frank L. Smith. *The Language of the Classroom*. New York: Teachers College Press, 1966.

Bellack, Arno A. "Methods for Observing Classroom Behavior of Teachers and Students." Unpublished paper, 1968. (Mimeographed.)

Biddle, B. J. and R. S. Adams. *An Analysis of Classroom Activities*. Columbia: Center for Research in Social Behavior, University of Missouri, 1967.

Boyd, Robert D. and M. Vere DeVault. "The Observation and Recording of Behavior." *Review of Educational Research*, XXXVI (December 1966), 529–551.

Bruner, Jerome S. *The Process of Education*. Cambridge, Massachusetts: Harvard University Press, 1963.

———. *On Knowing: Essays for the Left Hand*. Cambridge, Massachusetts: Belknap Press of Harvard University Press, 1963.

———. *Toward a Theory of Instruction*. Cambridge, Massachusetts: Belknap Press of Harvard University Press, 1966.

Cogan, Morris L. "Research on the Behavior of Teachers: A New Phase." *Journal of Teacher Education*, XIV (September 1963), 238–243.

———. "Theory and Design of a Study of Teacher-Pupil Interaction." *Harvard Educational Review*, XXVI (Fall 1956), 315–342.

Cornell, Francis G., Charles M. Lindvall, and Joe L. Saupe. *An Exploratory Measurement of Individualities of Schools and Classrooms.* Urbana: Bureau of Educational Research, University of Illinois, 1952.

Flanders, Ned A. *Teacher Influence, Pupil Attitudes, and Achievement.* U.S. Department of Health, Education, and Welfare, Office of Education, Cooperative Research Monograph No. 12. Washington, D.C.: U.S. Government Printing Office, 1965.

Gage, N. L. "An Analytic Approach to Research on Instructional Methods." *Phi Delta Kappan*, XLIX (June 1968), 601–606.

———. "Research on Cognitive Aspects of Teaching." *The Way Teaching Is: A Report of the Seminar on Teaching*. Washington, D.C.: Association for Supervision and Curriculum Development and National Education Association, 1966.

Galloway, Charles M. "An Exploratory Study of Observational Procedures for Determining Teacher Nonverbal Communication." Unpublished doctoral dissertation, University of Florida, 1962.

———. "Nonverbal Communication." *The Instructor*, LXXVII (April 1968), 37–42.

———. "Nonverbal Communication in Teaching." *Teaching: Vantage Points for Study*. Edited by Ronald T. Hyman. New York: J. B. Lippincott Company, 1968.

———. *Teaching Is Communicating: Nonverbal Language in the Classroom.* (Bulletin No. 29.) Washington, D.C.: The Association for Student Teaching, National Education Association, 1970.

Gauger, Paul W. "The Effect of Gesture and the Presence or Absence of Speaker on the Listening Comprehension of Eleventh and Twelfth Grade High School Pupils." Contained in "Abstracts of Theses in the Field of Speech and Drama, VII." Edited by Clyde W. Dow. *Speech Monographs*, XIX (March 1952), 116–117.

Grant, Barbara M. "A Method for Analyzing the Non-verbal Behavior (Physical Motions) of Teachers of Elementary School Language Arts." Unpublished doctoral dissertation, Teachers College, Columbia University, 1969.

Harrington, S. M. "Smiling as a Measure of Teacher Effectiveness." *Journal of Educational Research*, XLVIII (May 1955), 715–717.

Hughes, Marie M. *A Research Report: Assessment of the Quality of Teaching in Elementary Schools*. Salt Lake City: University of Utah Press, 1959.

Jackson, Phillip W. "The Way Teaching Is." *The Way Teaching Is: A Report of the Seminar on Teaching.* Washington, D.C.: Association for Supervision and Curriculum Development and the National Education Association, 1966.

Jayne, Clarence D. "A Study of the Relationship between Teaching Procedures and Educational Outcomes." *Journal of Experimental Education,* XIV (December 1945), 101–134.

Macdonald, James B. "The Person in the Curriculum." *Precedents and Promise in the Curriculum Field.* Edited by Helen F. Robinson. New York: Teachers College Press, 1966.

Medley, Donald M. and Harold E. Mitzel. "Application of Analysis of Variance to the Estimation of Reliability of Observations of Teachers' Classroom Behavior." *Journal of Experimental Education,* XXVII (September 1958), 23–25.

———. "Measuring Classroom Behavior by Systematic Observation." *Handbook of Research on Teaching,* Chapter IV. Edited by N. L. Gage. Chicago: Rand McNally and Co., 1963.

———. "A Technique for Measuring Classroom Behavior." *Journal of Educational Psychology,* XLIX (April 1958), 86–92.

Morsh, J. E. *Development Report: Systematic Observation of Instructor Behavior.* USAF Personnel Training Research Center Development Report, No. AFPTRC-TN-56-52, May 1956.

Perkins, H. V. "Classroom Behavior and Underachievement." *American Educational Research Journal,* II (January 1965), 1–12.

———. "A Procedure for Assessing the Classroom Behavior of Students and Teachers." *American Educational Research Journal,* I (November 1964), 249–260.

Rosenshine, Barak. "Behavioral Predictors of Effectiveness in Explaining Social Studies Material." Unpublished doctoral dissertation, Stanford University, 1968.

———. "To Explain: A Review of Research." *Educational Leadership,* XXVI (December 1968), 303–310.

Scheffler, Israel. *The Language of Education.* Springfield, Illinois: Charles C. Thomas, Publisher, 1964.

Silberman, Harry F., editor. "A Symposium on Current Research on Classroom Behavior of Teachers and Its Implications for Teacher Education." *Journal of Teacher Education,* XVI (September 1963), 235–237.

Smith, B. O. "A Concept of Teaching." *Teachers College Record,* LXI (February 1960), 229–241.

Smith, B. Othanel and Milton O. Meux, in collaboration with Jerrold Coombs, Daniel Eierdam, and Ronald Szoke. *A Study of the Logic of Teaching*. Urbana: Bureau of Educational Research, University of Illinois, 1962.

Smith, Louis M. and William Geoffrey. *The Complexities of an Urban Classroom: An Analysis toward a General Theory of Teaching*. New York: Holt, Rinehart and Winston, Inc., 1968.

Sullivan, George. *The Image of the Effective Teacher*. New York: The Central School Study, 1962.

Withall, John. "Development of a Technique for the Measurement of Socio-emotional Climate in Classrooms." *Journal of Experimental Education*, XVIII (March 1949), 347–361.

## RESEARCH AND STATISTICAL METHODS

Davitz, Joel R. and Lois Jean Davitz. *A Guide for Evaluating Research Plans in Psychology and Education*. New York: Teachers College Press, 1967.

Good, Carter V. and Douglas E. Scates. *Methods of Research*. New York: Appleton-Century-Crofts, Inc., 1954.

Kerlinger, Fred N. *Foundations of Behavioral Research*. New York: Holt, Rinehart and Winston, Inc., 1967.

Kuhn, Thomas S. *The Structure of Scientific Revolution*. Chicago: The University of Chicago Press, 1962.

Siu, R. G. H. *The Tao of Science*. Cambridge, Massachusetts: The M.I.T. Press, 1957.

Van Dalen, Theobold B. and William J. Meyer. *Understanding Educational Research*. New York: McGraw-Hill Book Company, 1966.

Walker, Helen M. and Joseph Lev. *Elementary Statistical Methods*. Revised edition. New York: Henry Holt and Company, 1958.

# Appendix A

# *Statistical Tables*

TABLE A-1. COEFFICIENT OF AGREEMENT BETWEEN TWO TEAMS CODING PHYSICAL MOTION *

| Category | Coefficient of Agreement ($R_i$) |
|---|---|
| *Instructional* | |
| Conducting | .970 |
|     Controlling Participation | .962 |
|     Obtaining Attending Behavior | .896 |
| Acting | .940 |
|     Emphasizing | .921 |
|     Illustrating | .916 |
|     Role Playing | 1.00 |
| Wielding | .952 |
|     Direct | .884 |
|     Indirect | .862 |
|     Instrumental | .800 |
| *Personal* | .995 |

* Each of the two teams comprised two individuals.

TABLE A-2. INSTRUCTIONAL AND PERSONAL MOTIONS USED BY CASE STUDY TEACHERS *

| Teacher | Total Number | Instructional | Personal |
|---|---|---|---|
| Mrs. Walker | 521 | 378<br>72.6% | 143<br>27.4% |
| Mrs. Higgins | 403 | 322<br>79.9% | 81<br>20.1% |
| Miss Straton | 436 | 394<br>90.4% | 42<br>9.6% |
| Mr. Rosen | 594 | 467<br>78.6% | 127<br>21.4% |
| Mr. Lambreck | 671 | 485<br>72.3% | 186<br>27.7% |
| Average | 525 | 409.2<br>77.9% | 115.8<br>22.1% |

* Five two-minute segments of teaching were used for each teacher.

TABLE A-3. INSTRUCTIONAL PHYSICAL MOTIONS USED BY CASE STUDY TEACHERS *

| Teacher | Total | Conducting | Acting | Wielding |
|---|---|---|---|---|
| Mrs. Walker | 378 | 230<br>60.8% | 31<br>8.2% | 117<br>31.0% |
| Mrs. Higgins | 322 | 262<br>81.4% | 29<br>9.0% | 31<br>9.6% |
| Miss Straton | 394 | 240<br>60.9% | 15<br>3.8% | 139<br>35.3% |
| Mr. Rosen | 467 | 258<br>55.2% | 82<br>17.6% | 127<br>27.2% |
| Mr. Lambreck | 485 | 289<br>59.6% | 22<br>4.5% | 174<br>35.9% |
| Average | 409.2 | 255.8<br>62.5% | 35.8<br>8.8% | 117.6<br>28.7% |

* Five two-minute segments of teaching were used for each teacher.

TABLE A-4. PHYSICAL MOTIONS PER CATEGORY THAT SERVE OR FACILITATE A PEDAGOGICAL FUNCTION*

| Teacher | Total NV/S | Total NV/F | Conducting NV/S | Conducting NV/F | Acting NV/S | Acting NV/F | Wielding NV/S | Wielding NV/F |
|---|---|---|---|---|---|---|---|---|
| Mrs. Walker | 49 13.0% | 329 87.0% | 43 18.7% | 187 81.3% | 0 | 31 100.0% | 6 5.1% | 111 94.9% |
| Mrs. Higgins | 49 15.2% | 273 84.8% | 42 16.7% | 220 84.0% | 5 17.2% | 24 82.8% | 2 6.5% | 29 93.5% |
| Miss Straton | 51 12.9% | 343 87.1% | 50 20.8% | 190 79.2% | 0 | 15 100.0% | 1 0.7% | 138 99.3% |
| Mr. Rosen | 70 15.0% | 397 85.0% | 65 25.2% | 193 74.8% | 0 | 82 100.0% | 5 3.9% | 122 96.1% |
| Mr. Lambreck | 49 10.1% | 436 89.9% | 42 14.5% | 247 85.5% | 0 | 22 100.0% | 7 4.0% | 167 96.0% |
| Average | 53.6 13.1% | 355.6 86.9% | 48.4 18.9% | 207.4 81.1% | 1 2.8% | 34.8 97.2% | 4.2 3.6% | 113.4 96.4% |

* Five two-minute segments of teaching were used for each of the case study teachers.

TABLE A-5. VERBAL MOTIONS AND NON-VERBAL MOTIONS THAT SERVE A PEDAGOGICAL FUNCTION *

| Teacher | Total Number of Motions that Serve | Verbal Motions that Serve | Non-verbal Motions that Serve |
|---|---|---|---|
| Mrs. Walker | 145 | 96<br>66.2% | 49<br>33.8% |
| Mrs. Higgins | 174 | 125<br>71.8% | 49<br>28.2% |
| Miss Straton | 168 | 117<br>69.6% | 51<br>30.4% |
| Mr. Rosen | 164 | 94<br>57.3% | 70<br>42.7% |
| Mr. Lambreck | 207 | 158<br>76.3% | 49<br>23.7% |
| Average | 171.6 | 118<br>68.8% | 53.6<br>31.2% |

* Five two-minute segments of teaching were used for each of the case study teachers.

TABLE A-6. MOVES SERVING DIFFERENT PEDAGOGICAL FUNCTIONS *

| Teacher | Total Motions that Serve | Structuring | Soliciting | Responding | Reacting |
|---|---|---|---|---|---|
| Mrs. Walker | 145 | 13<br>9.0% | 91<br>62.7% | 3<br>2.1% | 38<br>26.2% |
| Mrs. Higgins | 174 | 13<br>7.5% | 108<br>62.1% | 2<br>1.1% | 51<br>29.3% |
| Miss Straton | 168 | 2<br>1.2% | 107<br>63.7% | 3<br>1.8% | 56<br>33.3% |
| Mr. Rosen | 164 | 17<br>10.4% | 110<br>67.1% | 9<br>5.5% | 28<br>17.0% |
| Mr. Lambreck | 207 | 20<br>9.7% | 146<br>70.5% | 5<br>2.4% | 36<br>17.4% |
| Average | 171.6 | 13<br>7.6% | 112.4<br>65.5% | 4.4<br>2.6% | 41.8<br>24.3% |

* Five two-minute segments of teaching were used for each case study teacher.

TABLE A-7. NON-VERBAL MOTIONS SERVING DIFFERENT PEDAGOGICAL FUNCTIONS *

| Teacher | Total Non-verbal Motions that Serve | Structuring | Soliciting | Responding | Reacting |
|---|---|---|---|---|---|
| Mrs. Walker | 49 | 6<br>12.2% | 38<br>77.6% | 1<br>2.0% | 4<br>8.2% |
| Mrs. Higgins | 49 | 6<br>12.2% | 29<br>59.2% | 0 | 14<br>28.6% |
| Miss Straton | 51 | 0 | 34<br>66.7% | 0 | 17<br>33.3% |
| Mr. Rosen | 70 | 1<br>1.4% | 64<br>91.5% | 0 | 5<br>7.1% |
| Mr. Lambreck | 49 | 6<br>12.3% | 42<br>85.7% | 0 | 1<br>2.0% |
| Average | 53.6 | 3.8<br>7.1% | 41.4<br>77.2% | 0.2<br>0.4% | 8.2<br>15.3% |

* Five two-minute segments of teaching were used for each case study teacher.

TABLE A-8. VERBAL MOTIONS THAT SERVE DIFFERENT PEDAGOGICAL FUNCTIONS *

| Teacher | Total Verbal Motions that Serve | Structuring | Soliciting | Responding | Reacting |
|---|---|---|---|---|---|
| Mrs. Walker | 96 | 7<br>7.3% | 53<br>55.2% | 2<br>2.1% | 34<br>35.4% |
| Mrs. Higgins | 125 | 7<br>5.6% | 79<br>63.2% | 2<br>1.6% | 37<br>29.6% |
| Miss Straton | 117 | 2<br>1.7% | 73<br>62.4% | 3<br>2.6% | 39<br>33.3% |
| Mr. Rosen | 94 | 16<br>17.0% | 46<br>48.9% | 9<br>9.6% | 23<br>24.5% |
| Mr. Lambreck | 158 | 14<br>8.9% | 104<br>65.8% | 5<br>3.2% | 35<br>22.1% |
| Average | 118 | 9.2<br>7.8% | 71<br>60.2% | 4.2<br>3.5% | 33.6<br>28.5% |

* Five two-minute segments of teaching were used for each case study teacher.

TABLE A-9. MOVE PATTERNS USED BY CASE STUDY TEACHERS *

| Teacher | Move Patterns | | | | |
| --- | --- | --- | --- | --- | --- |
| | A<br>Verbal/Non-verbal | B<br>Verbal | C<br>Abortive | D<br>Non-verbal/Non-verbal | E<br>Non-verbal |
| Mrs. Walker | 90<br>62.1% | 6<br>4.1% | 0 | 15<br>10.3% | 34<br>23.5% |
| Mrs. Higgins | 106<br>60.9% | 19<br>10.9% | 0 | 26<br>15.0% | 23<br>13.2% |
| Miss Straton | 110<br>65.5% | 7<br>4.2% | 0 | 8<br>4.7% | 43<br>25.6% |
| Mr. Rosen | 85<br>51.8% | 9<br>5.5% | 0 | 24<br>14.6% | 46<br>28.1% |
| Mr. Lambreck | 128<br>61.8% | 29<br>14.0% | 1<br>0.5% | 15<br>7.3% | 34<br>16.4% |
| Average | 103.8<br>60.5% | 14<br>8.2% | 0.2<br>0.1% | 17.6<br>10.2% | 36<br>21.0% |

* Five two-minute segments of teaching were used for each teacher.

Appendix B

# An Inventory for Analyzing Non-verbal Teacher Activity

This inventory is to be used by teachers and student teachers to develop an awareness of how they function non-verbally in the classroom and of the many non-verbal options available to them. Each teacher completes the inventory either by recalling his own typical classroom behavior or by reviewing his activity as recorded on video tape. The teacher who completes the inventory by recalling his non-verbal behavior should not fill in the form in one sitting, but should read several of the questions, keep them in mind during several teaching sessions, and *then* react to those questions on the inventory.

There are no right or wrong answers, because it is impossible to say, for instance, that a particular way of illustrating or of indicating participants is the best. The teacher who answers each of the questions develops a profile of the kinds of motions he tends to use, the relationship between his non-verbal and verbal activity, and the characteristics of his motions. By developing a heightened awareness of his non-verbal functioning and of the possible non-verbal options available to him, hopefully the teacher will begin to use motion purposefully to achieve specific ends and will gain in effectiveness.

In Parts I and II, read each question and mark each motion indicating whether it is *very typical, typical,* or *atypical* of your classroom behavior. If there are other similar behaviors that you employ, list them on the lines marked "other." In Part III place an "X" indicating where you would place yourself on the various continua. After completing the inventory, study your answers to see if you can identify consistent patterns in your behavior.

# PART I

What kinds of motions tend to predominate in my non-verbal teaching style?

### A. *Conducting*

How do I control participation, focus attention, and obtain attending behavior?

|  | *Very Typical* | *Typical* | *Atypical* |
|---|---|---|---|
| 1. To indicate who the participant is, I: | | | |
| smile at the participant | ___ | ___ | ___ |
| focus my eyes on the participant | ___ | ___ | ___ |
| orient my body in the direction of the participant | ___ | ___ | ___ |
| nod at the chosen participant | ___ | ___ | ___ |
| point at the participant with finger, hand, stick, chalk, microphone, book | ___ | ___ | ___ |
| walk toward the participant | ___ | ___ | ___ |
| hand the pointer, chalk, book, microphone to the participant | ___ | ___ | ___ |
| touch the participant | ___ | ___ | ___ |
| other: _____ | ___ | ___ | ___ |

| | | | |
|---|---|---|---|
| 2. To rate a student's participation, I: | | | |
| use facial expressions: smiling, frowning, grinning, wrinkling my brow, raising my eyebrows | ___ | ___ | ___ |
| shake my head | ___ | ___ | ___ |
| shrug my shoulders | ___ | ___ | ___ |
| clap my hands | ___ | ___ | ___ |
| make the O.K. sign with my fingers, forming an "O" by touching thumb to forefinger | ___ | ___ | ___ |
| put my hands to my face | ___ | ___ | ___ |
| hold my head | ___ | ___ | ___ |
| scratch my head | ___ | ___ | ___ |
| write the correct response on the board or on a chart | ___ | ___ | ___ |
| pat student on back | ___ | ___ | ___ |
| move my hand from respondent to another student who has hand up to respond | ___ | ___ | ___ |

# An Inventory for Analyzing Non-verbal Teacher Activity

|  | Very Typical | Typical | Atypical |
|---|---|---|---|
| other: _____ | ___ | ___ | ___ |

3. To respond to a student's participation, I:
   |  | Very Typical | Typical | Atypical |
   |---|---|---|---|
   | use facial expressions | ___ | ___ | ___ |
   | shake or nod head | ___ | ___ | ___ |
   | walk toward or away from the participant | ___ | ___ | ___ |
   | point or wave hand | ___ | ___ | ___ |
   | write something on the board | ___ | ___ | ___ |
   | other: _____ | ___ | ___ | ___ |

4. To regulate the speed of classroom interaction, I:
   |  | Very Typical | Typical | Atypical |
   |---|---|---|---|
   | beckon to child to continue | ___ | ___ | ___ |
   | wave at child to stop | ___ | ___ | ___ |
   | wave at child to speed up | ___ | ___ | ___ |
   | select motions of different speeds | ___ | ___ | ___ |
   | other: _____ | ___ | ___ | ___ |

5. To focus student attention on a significant point in the lesson, I:
   |  | Very Typical | Typical | Atypical |
   |---|---|---|---|
   | write the significant point on the board | ___ | ___ | ___ |
   | underline a word or words written on the board | ___ | ___ | ___ |
   | point to each word written on the board | ___ | ___ | ___ |
   | write over each word written on the board, perhaps with colored chalk | ___ | ___ | ___ |
   | point to a related chart, bulletin board display, or picture | ___ | ___ | ___ |
   | point to a location on map or globe | ___ | ___ | ___ |
   | point to the actual object | ___ | ___ | ___ |
   | hold up the actual object | ___ | ___ | ___ |
   | point to a person being discussed | ___ | ___ | ___ |
   | point to a picture or statement projected by an audio-visual device | ___ | ___ | ___ |
   | put words or letters into a pocket chart | ___ | ___ | ___ |
   | attach word cards or pictures to the chalk board using magnets or masking tape | ___ | ___ | ___ |
   | hold up word card or picture | ___ | ___ | ___ |
   | add the key ingredient to a demonstration I am doing | ___ | ___ | ___ |
   | other: _____ | ___ | ___ | ___ |

128 THE TEACHER MOVES

|  | Very Typical | Typical | Atypical |
|---|---|---|---|
| 6. To get the attention of the total class or a portion of the class, I: | | | |
| close the door to indicate the lesson is beginning | ___ | ___ | ___ |
| flick the lights | ___ | ___ | ___ |
| tap a desk bell | ___ | ___ | ___ |
| pull down a chart or map | ___ | ___ | ___ |
| pick up a text book or lesson plan book or record book | ___ | ___ | ___ |
| walk to the front-center of room | ___ | ___ | ___ |
| survey the class, making eye contact | ___ | ___ | ___ |
| stand at attention | ___ | ___ | ___ |
| hold up my hand | ___ | ___ | ___ |
| play a note on the piano | ___ | ___ | ___ |
| arrange my chair or stool and sit down | ___ | ___ | ___ |
| tap fingers or pencil on desk | ___ | ___ | ___ |
| other: _____ | ___ | ___ | ___ |
| 7. To get the attention of a misbehaving child or group of children, I: | | | |
| orient my body toward and focus my eyes on the inattentive student(s) | ___ | ___ | ___ |
| frown or raise eyebrows at misbehaving student(s) | ___ | ___ | ___ |
| make hand gestures at the student(s) | ___ | ___ | ___ |
| shake my head at the misbehaving student(s) | ___ | ___ | ___ |
| snap fingers in direction of misbehaving student(s) | | | |
| clap hands | ___ | ___ | ___ |
| walk toward the misbehaving student(s) | ___ | ___ | ___ |
| touch misbehaving student(s) | ___ | ___ | ___ |
| sit down near misbehaving student(s) | ___ | ___ | ___ |
| touch object misbehaving student is touching | ___ | ___ | ___ |
| other: _____ | ___ | ___ | ___ |

## B. Acting

How do I use bodily motion to clarify and amplify meanings?

1. To emphasize meanings, I:
    use motions of my head          ___   ___   ___

## An Inventory for Analyzing Non-verbal Teacher Activity 129

|  | Very Typical | Typical | Atypical |
|---|---|---|---|
| use facial expressions | ___ | ___ | ___ |
| use motions of my hands | ___ | ___ | ___ |
| use motions of my feet | ___ | ___ | ___ |
| use motions of my entire body | ___ | ___ | ___ |
| other: _____ | ___ | ___ | ___ |

2. To illustrate a concept, an object, or a process, I:

| | | | |
|---|---|---|---|
| use motions of my hands | ___ | ___ | ___ |
| use motions of my head | ___ | ___ | ___ |
| use facial expressions | ___ | ___ | ___ |
| use motions of my feet | ___ | ___ | ___ |
| other: _____ | ___ | ___ | ___ |

3. To illustrate even more completely, I use role playing motions to:

| | | | |
|---|---|---|---|
| pretend I am an object | ___ | ___ | ___ |
| imitate an animal | ___ | ___ | ___ |
| pretend I am a particular character | ___ | ___ | ___ |
| pretend I am a puppet character | ___ | ___ | ___ |
| other: _____ | ___ | ___ | ___ |

### C. Wielding

In what ways do I manipulate objects, materials, or other parts of the environment when children are not expected to focus on my motions? What kinds of materials do I tend to manipulate?

1. I tend to manipulate:

| | | | |
|---|---|---|---|
| chalk and chalk board | ___ | ___ | ___ |
| books or workbooks | ___ | ___ | ___ |
| audio-visual equipment | ___ | ___ | ___ |
| paper, pens, or pencils | ___ | ___ | ___ |
| flow pens and charting paper | ___ | ___ | ___ |
| pictures or cards | ___ | ___ | ___ |
| materials related specifically to the teaching of my discipline | ___ | ___ | ___ |
| other: _____ | ___ | ___ | ___ |

2. During the lesson, I focus my eyes on written materials:

130   THE TEACHER MOVES

|  | Very Typical | Typical | Atypical |
|---|---|---|---|
| my lesson plans | ___ | ___ | ___ |
| the teacher's manual | ___ | ___ | ___ |
| the students' books | ___ | ___ | ___ |
| reference books | ___ | ___ | ___ |
| material recorded on chalkboard | ___ | ___ | ___ |
| numerals of the clock | ___ | ___ | ___ |
| other: _____ | ___ | ___ | ___ |

3. Teacher-oriented wieldings I delegate to students are:

|  | Very Typical | Typical | Atypical |
|---|---|---|---|
| distribution and collection of materials | ___ | ___ | ___ |
| setting up equipment | ___ | ___ | ___ |
| putting material on board or bulletin board | ___ | ___ | ___ |
| reading questions that other students answer | ___ | ___ | ___ |
| other: _____ | ___ | ___ | ___ |

4. I manipulate or wield materials:

|  | Very Typical | Typical | Atypical |
|---|---|---|---|
| before students come into the room | ___ | ___ | ___ |
| while students come into the room | ___ | ___ | ___ |
| while students are performing some other task | ___ | ___ | ___ |
| just before using the material | ___ | ___ | ___ |
| during the actual use of the material | ___ | ___ | ___ |
| other: _____ | ___ | ___ | ___ |

### D. Personal Motions

How do I use motions that are more of a personal nature than they are instructional?

1. Motions I make that are related to my clothing are:

|  | Very Typical | Typical | Atypical |
|---|---|---|---|
| adjusting my tie or bow | ___ | ___ | ___ |
| adjusting my collar | ___ | ___ | ___ |
| straightening jacket | ___ | ___ | ___ |
| pulling down sweater or skirt | ___ | ___ | ___ |
| tucking in blouse, sweater, or shirt | ___ | ___ | ___ |
| other: _____ | ___ | ___ | ___ |

# An Inventory for Analyzing Non-verbal Teacher Activity 131

|  | Very Typical | Typical | Atypical |
|---|---|---|---|
| 2. Motions I make in the classroom that are aspects of my own personality are: | | | |
| pushing back hair | ___ | ___ | ___ |
| pulling on beads, necklace, locket, tie | ___ | ___ | ___ |
| adjusting glasses | ___ | ___ | ___ |
| placing hands in pockets | ___ | ___ | ___ |
| jiggling coins in pocket | ___ | ___ | ___ |
| twiddling with ring | ___ | ___ | ___ |
| curling hair around finger | ___ | ___ | ___ |
| scratching head, nose, neck, leg | ___ | ___ | ___ |
| other: _____ | ___ | ___ | ___ |

3. My physical motions that might be called mannerisms because I repeatedly make them are:

_____  ___  ___  ___

_____

## PART II

How does my non-verbal activity relate to my verbal activity?

1. To communicate meaning, I use non-verbal motion without any verbal accompaniment   ___  ___  ___
2. I use non-verbal motion in my classroom to support my verbal remarks   ___  ___  ___
3. I use non-verbal motion in my classroom to support other non-verbal activity   ___  ___  ___
4. I use verbal remarks without non-verbal accompaniment   ___  ___  ___

## PART III

How do I carry on classroom activity? I generally:

| | | | |
|---|---|---|---|
| sit at the teacher's desk | ___ | ___ | ___ |
| sit on the teacher's desk | ___ | ___ | ___ |
| sit on stool | ___ | ___ | ___ |
| sit on a student's chair | ___ | ___ | ___ |
| sit on a student's desk | ___ | ___ | ___ |
| sit on floor | ___ | ___ | ___ |
| lean on the chalk board | ___ | ___ | ___ |
| lean on a desk | ___ | ___ | ___ |

132  THE TEACHER MOVES

|  | Very Typical | Typical | Atypical |
|---|---|---|---|
| stand at the front of room | ____ | ____ | ____ |
| stand at the side or rear of room | ____ | ____ | ____ |
| move up and down the aisles | ____ | ____ | ____ |
| move from group to group | ____ | ____ | ____ |
| move from child to child | ____ | ____ | ____ |
| move across the front of room | ____ | ____ | ____ |
| move from desk to chalk board | ____ | ____ | ____ |
| move around the outside edge of room | ____ | ____ | ____ |
| sit at a table with the students | ____ | ____ | ____ |
| other: _____ | ____ | ____ | ____ |

## PART IV

What are the general characteristics of my non-verbal classroom behavior?

### A. *Activity Level*

Consider the number of non-verbal clues you tend to generate in a classroom. Are you very active, active, not too active? Plot yourself on the following activity continuum:

```
very active            active              not too active
|----------------------|------------------------------|
```

### B. *Speed of Motion*

Consider the non-verbal motions you make in the classroom. Do you tend to move rapidly? Do you tend to move rather slowly? Plot yourself on the following speed continuum:

```
rapid                  medium                    slow
|----------------------|------------------------------|
```

### C. *Size of Motion*

Consider the non-verbal motions you make. Do you tend to make such large motions as broad gestures of the hand? Or do you tend to make such small motions as a nod or smile? Plot yourself on the following size continuum:

```
large                  medium                   small
|----------------------|------------------------------|
```

### D. Personal Motions

Consider the personal motions you use in a classroom. Do you use many personal motions? Do you use a minimal number of personal motions? Plot yourself on the following continuum:

```
many personal motions          few personal motions
|_____|_____|
```

### E. Verbal/Non-verbal Orientation

Consider the non-verbal activity and the verbal activity that you carry on in the classroom. Do you have a non-verbal orientation in your teaching? Do you have a verbal orientation? Plot yourself on the following verbal/non-verbal continuum:

```
verbal          verbal/non-verbal          non-verbal
|_____|_____|
```

### F. Clarity of Communication

Consider these questions:
    Is my bodily stance communicating what I want it to communicate?
    Is my manner of sitting communicating what I want it to communicate?
    Is my manner of walking communicating what I want it to communicate?
    Is my gesturing communicating what I want to communicate?
    Are my facial expressions communicating what I want to communicate?
In terms of these questions plot yourself on the following clarity of communication continuum:

```
motion communicates what        motion does not
     is intended            communicate what is intended
|_____|_____|
```